LOST GARDENS
OF ENGLAND

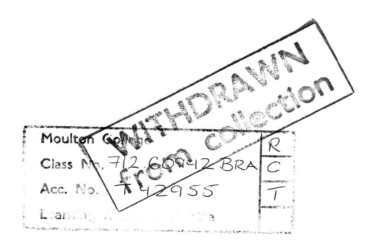

LOST GARDENS OF ENGLAND

FROM THE ARCHIVES OF COUNTRY LIFE

KATHRYN BRADLEY-HOLE

AURUM PRESS

First published in Great Britain 2004 by Aurum Press Limited
25 Bedford Avenue, London WC1B 3AT

Design by James Campus
Originated by Colorlito-CST Srl, Milan
Printed and bound in Singapore by CS Graphics

Frontispiece: *The Round Pond and temple at Gunnersbury Park, Middlesex, photographed in 1900.*
Front endpaper: *The terraces at Lilleshall, Shropshire, with Victorian rustic tree seat.*
Rear endpaper: *Lord Lonsdale's busts at Campsea Ashe, Suffolk.*

THE COUNTRY LIFE PICTURE LIBRARY

The *Country Life* Picture Library holds a complete set of prints made from its negatives, and a card index to the subjects, usually recording the name of the photographer and the date of the photographs catalogued, together with a separate index of photographers. It also holds a complete set of *Country Life* and various forms of published indices to the magazine. The Library may be visited by appointment, and prints of any negatives it holds can be supplied by post.

For further information, please contact the Librarian, Camilla Costello, at *Country Life*, King's Reach Tower, Stamford Street, London SE1 9LS (*Tel:* 020 7261 6337).

ACKNOWLEDGEMENTS

My sincere thanks to my colleagues at *Country Life*: Clive Aslet, the editor, Michael Hall, the deputy editor and series editor for *Country Life* books, and Camilla Costello, the custodian of the photographic library, all of whom have given the utmost encouragement and enthusiasm to the project. Also to my editors at Aurum Press, Clare Howell and Karen Ings, who have worked with great care and patience, and the book's designer, James Campus, whose creative and discerning eye has made the very best use of the wonderful photographs.

I am also most grateful to the numerous people who have enthusiastically helped my researches and considerably broadened the scope of the book through the information they have been able to pass on, in particular the staff of the Royal Horticultural Society's Lindley Library, the County Records Offices, English Heritage, the Garden History Society and the Society of Gardens Trusts.

Many other individuals and institutions have kindly assisted me in my research, including the garden owners, agents, head gardeners and local historians whose immediate and intimate knowledge of the properties and their histories has been invaluable. I would particularly like to thank Mrs Astor, Kate and Rupert Atkin, Lord Beaverbrook, Anna Chambers, Christine Clarke, Claire and John Davison, Penelope Dawson-Brown, Charles Du Cane, Gareth Evans, Paula Fahey, Grant Fanjul, Roy and Pip Gardener, Christopher Gibbs, Inara Gipsler, Sandy Haynes, John Herbert, David Jacques, Shirley Lawrence, Audrey Le Lievre, Kerry McKenzie Smith, Michael Marshall, Valerie Martin, Steve Morrison, John Nuttall, Conrad Payne, Laura Platman, Chris Peace, Neil Porteous, Tricia Rickards, Lionel de Rothschild, Jane Seymour, Christopher Statham, Sir Roy Strong, Jenny Swingler, the University of Exeter, the University of Nottingham, Anderley Wade, Olive Waller and Jennifer White.

CONTENTS

GARDENS very easily become 'lost'. Unlike buildings, which, tempests, fire and earthquakes excepted, generally stay put and change little unless man intervenes, gardens are intrinsically restless. They are impatient to grow, to flower, set seed, retreat, regenerate and move off again in different forms. This, I think, is one of their great fascinations – that constant cycle of growth, maturity, death and renewal which occurs independently.

Like everything else that is organic, in the literal sense of the word, a garden has its own agenda, which will be implemented if allowed to run its course. For some of the gardens in this book, that is what happened: a steady, almost imperceptible metamorphosis took place over the space of a few generations. The neat hedges became massive trees; the deep shade the trees cast meant the flowers could no longer grow alongside them. After the carnage of the First World War, there were no longer platoons of gardeners attempting to hold back the tide of change, to maintain the status quo. And sometimes it was simply changes in fashion that demanded a new look.

Some of these gardens have not completely disappeared; the land is still there, parts of the infrastructure may be more or less intact, but the original intention and spirit have long departed and been replaced by something quite different. At Lindridge, for example, a reasonable chunk of a once magnificent garden survives after a fashion, and is cared for by its well-intentioned community, but it is no longer aligned on the central vista of a great house. Instead, it has become the incidental pleasant flower garden beside an estate of twenty-one new houses. The loss of context for a garden can be almost as devastating as its complete destruction.

Other gardens are comprehensively gone, whether scattered and buried under developments of housing, as at Esher Place in Surrey, or flattened and turned into a crematorium, as at Muntham Court in Sussex, or even smothered by a power station, as at Drakelowe Hall in Derbyshire. Norah Lindsay's garden at Sutton Courtenay lasted for the fifty-odd years when it was hers, then quickly vanished, to be replaced by a more modern and manageable design. In spite of that, her influence on country gardening style pervaded the rest of the twentieth century.

Yet there is certainly nothing new in the disappearance of gardens in this country and the underlying cause is not always reduced finances. In 1753, it was reported in *The World* magazine that gardens 'are usually new-created once in twenty or thirty years, and no traces left of their former condition'. We should not wonder at such alterations, advised the author: 'Were any man of taste not to lay out his ground in the style which prevailed less than half a century ago, it would occasion as much astonishment and laughter, as if a modern beau should appear in the drawing-room in red stockings.' This was written when Capability Brown was approaching the height of his fame, pushing naturalistic styles of landscape gardening further along the winding trails that had been fashioned so artistically by William Kent a generation before. That Humphry Repton's more mannered approach was to follow straight after, and to lead into the 'bold roughness of nature' prescribed by the Picturesque movement, exactly proves the point of *The World*'s observation.

By the time Queen Victoria came to the throne, the wheel had turned full circle, and English garden owners were ready for a return to the formality, symmetry and geometry that had preceded the landscape movement. Like its architecture, Victorian garden taste underwent several revivalist phases during the long reign of the Queen, facilitated by advances in glasshouse technology and the influx of a multitude of new plants arriving for the first time from far-off lands. Many of the great Victorian gardens were set-pieces on a grand scale, with stairways, balustrades and terraces in the Italian Renaissance style, and formal planting displays that showed off not only the wealth of the owner, but also, just as importantly, the horticultural expertise of the head gardener.

The glamorous weekly journal *Country Life Illustrated* (as it was called at first) was launched in the twilight of both the nineteenth century and Queen Victoria's reign. It was poised to take full advantage of the latest developments in landscape design and was to influence gardening taste for much of the twentieth century. Nevertheless, as some of the lost gardens in these pages show, the magazine's first issues appear to reflect earlier tastes in design, eulogising high-Victorian gardens that by the end of the century were widely perceived as throwbacks. Castle Ashby in Northamptonshire, for instance, with its elaborate parterre from the 1860s, was an anachronism in 1900 when it was featured in the magazine, as was the garden of St Catherine's Court, near Bath, with its beds cut like pastry shapes, which were regarded as 'quaint' in 1899.

Above: *Wondrous new plants were raised on the 30 acres of Veitch & Sons' Coombe Wood Nursery, supplying voracious Victorian gardeners.*

Left: *The boathouse and tranquil lake at Tortworth Court, Gloucestershire, in 1899, now a part of Leyhill Prison.*

The first edition of *Country Life* was published at the start of Queen Victoria's Diamond Jubilee year, on 8 January 1897, though apparently it was conceived on Walton Heath golf course a couple of years earlier by Edward Hudson, a printer and publisher. Hudson pooled resources with two other publishers, George (Lord) Riddell and Sir George Newnes, but it was Hudson who became the overall proprietor and, indeed, a powerful creative force whose unerring eye for a good photograph (printed to the highest standards) assured the magazine's success for its first three-and-a-half decades. (The story of the magazine's origins and first hundred years is eloquently told in Roy Strong's *Country Life 1897–1997: The English Arcadia*.)

Country Life set out to be 'The journal for all interested in country life and country pursuits', as its subtitle declared, covering the traditional field sports of hunting, shooting and fishing. There was also horse-racing (*Country Life Illustrated* emerged out of a well-produced but commercially unviable paper called *Racing Illustrated*).

An unpublished photograph of the Fig Court at Ashford Chace, Hampshire, built by Inigo Triggs and W. F. Unsworth in 1912 for the naturalist and explorer Aubyn Trevor-Battye.

Its highly pictorial format also included the newly popular (in England) game of golf and visually arresting items on rural life, especially country homes, gardening, wildlife and what might best be termed 'picturesque yokels'.

Christopher Hussey, who was the magazine's editor from 1933 to 1940 and a key player in its success for many years afterwards, noted: 'Hudson's flash of genius at Walton Heath was to connect the increasing number of people who, like himself, were escaping from towns (some of them in automobiles) to find country life and country homes, with the idea of providing a medium for well-presented advertisements of country residences.'

The Hudson connection is also vital because, in 1900, the great gardening pundit William Robinson sold to Hudson his interest in *The Garden*, a magazine which he had founded and edited since

1871, and to which Gertrude Jekyll, the well-known gardener and writer, had long contributed. (As a measure of Gertrude Jekyll's influence in the horticultural firmament, it should be noted that, in 1897, when sixty eminent gardeners were presented with a Victoria Medal of Honour, created by the Royal Horticultural Society to commemorate the Queen's Jubilee, she was one of only two women to receive it. The other was Ellen Willmott, of Warley Place.) Miss Jekyll was persuaded to edit *The Garden*, and also to supply regular gardening notes to *Country Life*. She, in turn, introduced Hudson to the young Edwin Lutyens, and this creative triumvirate, assisted by *Country Life*'s outstanding photographers, began to inform a rapidly growing number of house-owners how to create and plant their gardens; the Lutyens house with a Jekyll garden became a regular fixture in the magazine through the first two decades of the twentieth century.

In *Country Life* garden features, herbaceous borders, rock gardens, woodland gardens, pergolas and pavings all got the Jekyll treatment – and also reached a wider audience through a series of books that Jekyll published under the *Country Life* imprint. It was a highly satisfactory and symbiotic relationship, with the magazine benefiting from the latest fashionable designs of Lutyens and Jekyll, and they in turn reaping the rewards of regular exposure in the journal most likely to yield further client enquiries.

In its very early years, *Country Life*'s house and garden features were often elaborately worded yet thin on information, but always exquisitely photographed. For this we have to thank the magazine's celebrated photographers and, in particular, Charles Latham (who died in 1909). Latham's photographs, many of which are reproduced in this book, are unequalled for their hauntingly romantic depiction of the Edwardian 'golden afternoon', the *Go-Between* world that was lost forever with the outbreak of war in 1914. It was Latham who gave us the iconic 'lady by the lake' at Sedgwick Park; Latham's eye shows us the splendid vistas over the parterre at Castle Ashby, the picturesque quaintness of Cleeve Prior, and the extravagance of Easton Lodge. The gardener posed, somewhere off to right or left and going about his business, was certainly staged; yet such details invigorated these gardens with human life and toil, so that we see them not just as gardens but as the real-life stage wherein unglamorous lives were also being lived out. These were places where the greenhouses needed damping down in hot weather and the boilers needed to be stoked in the freezing night, onion sets had to be laid in precisely measured rows, apples to be espaliered, cucumbers straightened, grapes thinned, miles of hedges clipped by hand and grass raked up once the mowing team had trundled by.

To these haunting images, Edward Hudson also applied his strong visual sensibilities. As Roy Strong has pointed out, 'Hudson probably acted as some kind of picture editor ... sitting in his office looking at every picture, rejecting half of them. ... Whether it is a ploughman pushing his solitary furrow across a field, a frosted wood, a room in some ancient mansion or an aristocrat with her children, every picture exudes a lyrical romanticism. However varied the

Charles Latham, Country Life*'s celebrated photographer, captured Emma Henderson, the owner, by the rectangular pool and rock gardens of Sedgwick Park, Sussex, in 1900. The pool was called 'The White Sea'.*

subjects, the magazine visually reads as one and that could only have been achieved by the control of a single discerning eye.'

As time progressed, the writing on gardens developed to become an alluring counterpoint to the sumptuous illustrations. William Robinson added occasional articles, Miss Jekyll had a regular column, and the trickle of contributions by Henry Avray Tipping from 1903 onwards brought rigorous historical research into the frame. Tipping, a friend of the architect and garden designer Harold Peto, was also a consummate garden designer and edited the final volume of Latham's *Gardens Old and New* (1907).

In 1909, Lawrence Weaver joined the team, understudying Tipping in the coverage of country homes. Weaver instigated an invaluable series on 'Lesser Country Houses', usually relegated to the magazine's 'supplement' pages, where it did not need to compete

for space with the great houses but brought in lucrative advertising revenue related to new homes and home improvements. Yet it yielded some of the best features on contemporary homes, particularly many of Lutyens' houses and gardens, as well as other Arts and Crafts architects' work. One example was the architectural garden of Ashford Chace, designed by H. Inigo Triggs with W. F. Unsworth for the explorer Aubyn Trevor-Battye, which today, like so many others, is broken up into divided ownership.

The earliest *Country Life* photographs occasionally captured what are now 'lost' horticultural techniques, most obviously the horse- or donkey-drawn mowing machine, with a garden boy leading the harnessed animal and a journeyman gardener bringing up the rear end of the ensemble to guide the mower. On soft ground the horse would be required to wear special leather boots to protect the turf from becoming pitted with crescent-shaped hoof-prints. The latest steam-powered mowing machines were being used in some of the larger gardens around the turn of the twentieth century, and at Sudbourne Hall, which had one of the largest lawns in the country, not one but two steam mowers were regularly employed. Yet at Tortworth Court, a gardener was photographed scything the sward in a method that reverberates back through the centuries; scythe design has hardly changed since Roman times.

If a fine lawn, with all its necessary rolling and labour-intensive mowing, was a luxurious status symbol a century ago, then the turf stairway added another layer of cachet. It was 1914 when *Country Life* photographed the great grass stairway at Milton Abbas, Dorset – over a hundred crisply smooth turf steps rising with knife-edge precision between pristine hedges and neat little buttons and cones of topiary work. Although their care must have been compromised during the Great War, it is remarkable that the Milton Abbas steps still survive today, albeit in a far less manicured state and lacking the crisp hedge margins that helped to define the feature. Most turf stairs were long ago replaced by steps in hard materials, especially if the gradient was steep. The very charming nineteenth-century example

Below: *Like an attentive congregation with hymn books open, the hollyhocks of the Archbishop of Canterbury's garden at Lambeth Palace stand to attention.*

Right: *At Spains Hall, Essex, a well-trained donkey calmly mows the lawns. By 1900, some gardens were replacing horsepower with steam-driven machines.*

at St Catherine's Court (see page 36) is now only a lawn, though it ascends in waves where the steps used to lie.

Horticultural techniques were not often discussed in the features on specific gardens in the early decades, the subject of practical gardening being the domain of the weekly 'In The Garden' columns and seasonal articles, which for many years were written by Gertrude Jekyll. Topical practical features were also contributed by William Robinson, or sometimes by articulate head gardeners (such as Edwin Beckett VMH at Aldenham House, a star in his own right, and James Hudson VMH, Leopold de Rothschild's formidable head gardener at Gunnersbury).

Yet shafts of light were occasionally shone into the practical world that lay behind the glamorous photography. For example, at Compton End, G. H. Kitchin described all the shiftings and level-lings of soil necessary in order to lay out his pond garden. At Shepherd's Gate, Mrs Hutchinson was praised for the very high quality of her sweet peas and kitchen-garden produce (neither were photographed, alas, since kitchen gardens were seldom considered worthy of attention – a very unfortunate viewpoint, as it ignored the extraordinary focus on perfect produce and luxury fruits that was the pride of many a country house). Tantalisingly, Mrs Hutchinson's

At Westlands Farm, Lord Darnley's naturalistic planting of lupins created a modern-looking rainbow effect, especially with the broad mown path snaking through longer grass.

successes were put down to her personal interest in 'Nitro-bacterine', though no further explanation was given. And yet these were pioneering years for the fertiliser industry. Agricultural bacteriology in the late-nineteenth and early-twentieth centuries was making great strides since, for the first time, soil microbes were being seen by scientists as resources to be exploited and not simply as pests. The most efficient strains of useful bacteria were beginning to be cultivated and made available in agriculture and horticulture. Though we take it for granted today that certain soil bacteria assist in the acquisition and transformation of nitrogen compounds, Mrs Hutchinson's inoculations of her legume seeds with Nitro-bacterine were inspired by the very latest scientific developments in fertiliser research.

Sometimes it is suggested that a monoculture way of planting is a modern idea. It is not, of course. Devoting an entire section of your acreage to a single plant was much in vogue in the early twentieth century. Gertrude Jekyll believed every country home should have a Michaelmas daisy garden, though it might be in bloom for only three or four weeks in the year. Other contemporary enthusiasms were for iris gardens, peony gardens (Lawrence Johnston's peony garden at Hidcote Manor was photographed in 1930), lupin gardens (Lord Darnley arranged rainbow waves of lupins naturalistically at Westlands Farm), and, of course, the widely adopted dahlia garden, which was really a two-season garden since the dahlias would be taken out each autumn to be replaced by spring bulbs. One unusual monoculture captured by *Country Life* was a sea of hollyhocks beneath the ailanthus trees at Lambeth Palace in London. *Ailanthus altissima*, the 'tree of Heaven', naturally has a place in the garden of an Archbishop; the presence of *Alcea rosea* in such great quantity and variety is less easy to explain, but, as they were standing to attention like a most attentive congregation, perhaps they inspired the writing of sermons and letters.

The most constantly admired monoculture was, of course, the rose garden, which received extensive coverage during the Hudson years of influence. Outstanding and by now long-lost examples included the acres of roseries at Downside, near Leatherhead, and Shiplake Court in Berkshire (now a school); also, the most famous of all, Caunton Manor, ancestral home of Samuel Reynolds Hole, the Dean of Rochester who founded the (Royal) National Rose Society.

Many country gardens were defined by their trees, especially the majestic cedar of Lebanon (and, to a lesser extent, the deodar), which, since the days of Capability Brown, no house of any stature could be without. Among the most impressive were the cedars clustered around the house at Campsea Ashe in Suffolk, and those forming an avenue at Linton Hall, Kent, already mature in 1899 and now long gone. Somehow, tree losses are particularly hard to bear, all the more so when they once formed a great drive. Linton Hall, like Aldenham House, Campsea Ashe and countless other mansions, was approached a hundred years ago via an impressive avenue of mature elms leading up to the house. Nowadays, we can only look at drawings and photographs of those arboreal giants that dominated the English landscape, since the ravages of Dutch Elm disease through the 1970s radically speeded up a longer-term decline in the genus, consigning most of England's elms to history, at least for present generations. For some properties the loss of elms meant a serious loss of identity: The Wyck, at Hitchin, Hertfordshire, was an ancient cottage whose very name was inspired by the great wych elms that, for centuries, had sprung out of the hedgerows all around it in a pattern of constant regeneration.

Topiary had been diving in and out of fashion through the second half of the nineteenth century and, from the start, *Country Life* recorded an astonishing range of examples, from the extravagant crowns and gazebos of the Earl of Harrington's Elvaston Castle to numerous more humble figures chanced upon beside cottage doorways. In fact, topiary was so much a part of the magazine that from 1898 until 1940, the features on country houses and gardens were headed by a lavish panel designed in Art Nouveau mood by John Byam Shaw, depicting clipped trees and a topiary peacock surmounting a glorious banner, into which the headline text was inserted. Enchanting topiaries were photographed in every corner of Britain, from bulging pepperpots at Treworgey in Cornwall to the

A rare Edwardian photograph of the allotments created at the Royal Hospital, Chelsea, in the mid-nineteenth century to keep veterans out of the 'gin shops'. A new infirmary covered this plot in 1960.

great arcaded hedges of Muntham Court near the Sussex coast, and up into the baronial demesnes of Scotland. One of the most impressive topiary gardens was at Brockenhurst Park in the New Forest, which required far too much manual labour to thrive for long after the lifetime of its maker, though many of its hedges survive in plain form.

Topiary very much fitted into the *Country Life* ethos, since it was an integral part of many country-house grounds on the one hand, while on the other, it complemented the magazine's promotion of an unpretentious cottage-garden style, championed in the early years by Gertrude Jekyll. Yet it was not always a predictable art. Topiary is as idiosyncratic as the people who practise it and one of the most beguiling of *Country Life*'s lost gardens is a simple hard-working cottage garden whose boundary hedges of yew had been fashioned into wonderfully wrought displays of coiled cobras (see page 15). As this was Colonel Eden's cottage, the expectation is that it was inspired by years spent in army service overseas, in either India or Africa, though the full story has yet to be unravelled.

As a weekly journal mainly concerned with rural interests, *Country Life* has featured few town gardens. The exceptions in the early years arose mainly when the house belonged to someone famous – such as the artist Sir Lawrence Alma-Tadema – or when an architect had performed a stylish transformation and perhaps produced a plan. The garden at King's Head House, Buckinghamshire, was a good example of how a long but slender, wedge-shaped plot could be turned into a progression of ordered flowerbeds and paths with a central feature pool, uncluttered in the modern style.

Even rarer are pictures of allotments. At the Royal Hospital, Chelsea, the photographer sent to photograph the building indoors and out for an architectural feature also ventured into the pensioners'

In 1905, magnificent elm trees dominated the skyline around The Wyck, at Hitchin, Hertfordshire. The widespread loss of elms in the 1970s has drastically altered the English landscape.

Carnations and standard roses at Shepherd's Gate, among the hills of the Ashdown Forest in Sussex, photographed c.1909.

allotment grounds. Nearly a century on the unpublished pictures of Crimean War and Indian Mutiny veterans patiently nurturing their crops seem especially poignant. The original hospital allotments (in Ranelagh Gardens) were established in 1832 by Lord John Russell to tempt the veterans away from the considerable draw of 'the gin shops'. In 1859 they were moved to the Governor's and Physic Garden, where 144 plots survived for a hundred years until a new infirmary was built on the land in 1960.

Rock gardens – even in the middle of London – were occasionally photographed, and not just during the few heady days of the Chelsea Flower Show. One good example was a naturalistic moraine landscape of water-worn Westmorland limestone, transported to a stylish house in Holland Park and incongruously laid out between high walls of London stock bricks. More often, a town garden in the first half of the twentieth century was a fairly predictable composition of lawns, rose beds and perhaps a small herbaceous border; the paths were straight, usually crazy-paved and with little mats of thyme spilling out between the paving joints.

Most unusually, one fashionable crazy-paving garden of the between-the-wars period in a terraced row of houses was captured at teatime one summer's day, with a crowd of occupants gathered in their swimwear. The view, taken from an upstairs window, allows us glimpses of the neighbours' narrow plots on either side; the River Thames flows beyond, for this was the Hammersmith Terrace home of the writer A. P. Herbert, photographed in 1931 (see page 16). There is only one shot, perhaps taken for fun, for it appears not to have been published; the rest of the set is devoted to the interiors.

If town gardens were few and far between, then cottage gardens made up the deficit in the small-is-beautiful league. 'The present-day cottager exhibits a decided leaning towards the cultivation of purely decorative plants, such as sunflowers and hollyhocks, though he usually contrives to combine the ornamental with the useful,

by planting these gaudy flowers mixed among his vegetables,' observed a writer in November 1897. *Country Life*'s roses-round-the-door cottage pictures, with, perhaps, a tabby cat lapping at a dish nearby, were the photographic equivalent of Helen Allingham's watercolours, and, early on, 'Cottage Gardens of England' became an occasional series within the magazine. As well as providing views of 'Humble Homesteads' with creeper-covered thatch, they helped to inform owners of gardens both large and small of a bucolic and informal approach to planting, using simple hardy flowers rather than exotics cultivated with the expenses of a glasshouse. Jekyll's own high regard for cottagers and their gardens fanned the flames of a fashion for cottage-garden style which found favour in the new wave of second-home owners: the rapidly growing number of professional urban dwellers for whom a country cottage was becoming the ideal weekend retreat.

There was, however, one major contemporary garden trend that *Country Life* tried hard to ignore. Japanese gardens had become fashionable since trade had reopened with Japan after two centuries of closed borders. An influx of new plants (Veitch's Nursery had distributed Japanese plants in England since the 1860s) was joined by the publication in 1893 of Josiah Conder's *Landscape Gardening in Japan*. By the Edwardian era, Japanese gardens were very much in vogue, with Yokohama Nursery distributing an English-language catalogue of '*Iris Kaempferi, newest & rarest, 50 varieties*'. At Easton Lodge, the Countess of Warwick had her ceremonial tea-house installed at the water's edge, and other excellent early-twentieth-century examples still exist at Heale House, Wiltshire, and Tatton Park, Cheshire.

The image of the cottage gardener cultivating simple flowers was an enduring one, greatly encouraged by Gertrude Jekyll.

One of the most surprising gardens of the Edwardian era was that at Colonel Eden's cottage, enlivened by giant cobras snaking through the yew hedge.

In 1908, the aristocratic English sisters Florence and Ella Du Cane published *The Flowers and Gardens of Japan*, with fifty exquisite colour plates of painted scenes in Japanese gardens accompanied by a very readable analysis of their elements and iconography – the descriptions were laced with vivid travellers' tales. Paradoxically, while such gardens were all the rage in Europe, the Du Canes were recording a rapidly disappearing world. 'Unfortunately many of the finest specimens of landscape gardens, the old Daimyos' gardens in Tokyo, have been swept away to make room for foreign houses, factories, and breweries, and no trace of them remains,' wrote Florence Du Cane.

It is tempting to speculate that the Du Canes inspired Emma Henderson's refashioning of her Classical water garden at Sedgwick Park into an overtly Oriental scene, but Japanese styling was not embraced at *Country Life*. Lawrence Weaver wrote in 1915, 'The

importation of exotic motifs into garden design in England is dangerous not only because they are rarely understood, but because there are few sites where they can take their place at all naturally. The disposition of a few typical ornaments, of a bronze stork here and a stone lantern there, does not make a Japanese garden.' He drily observed that they merely made English gardens speak with a Japanese accent. Perhaps Christopher Hussey agreed, for when he wrote about the Du Canes' garden in 1925, he failed to mention the Japanese area by name, though it was clearly significant in the light of their work. He merely referred to a dell garden, which happened to contain some irises from Japan.

In this book, I have aimed to cover as broad a spectrum of lost English gardens as possible. Some already well-known examples, adequately covered in other books, were excluded in order to make space for new and unexplored material. We see within these pages a diverse collection of gardens that were photographed from the late 1890s up to the late 1930s – a period of only forty years, but a time of great social and economic upheaval during which many

great houses were demolished. Almost invariably, their gardens were lost too.

More recently, in the half-century since the end of the Second World War, new threats to gardens and parks came chiefly from the increased demand for arable farming, which resulted in the ploughing-up of ornamental grounds, and from property redevelopments, either for housing or business. We now need to add to this list of factors the deleterious effects of indiscriminate water abstraction and the ongoing results of climate change, which may significantly change more gardens by altering the types of plants able to thrive in specific locations. Various plant pathogens of a seriousness comparable to Dutch Elm disease may also adversely affect gardens in the future; indeed, a wave of fungal diseases of box plants, collectively known as box blights, has decimated box hedges and parterres in many of Britain's historic gardens in recent years, while *Phytophthora ramorum* (known in America as 'sudden oak death') is a recent arrival to our shores and has proved fatal to rhododendrons and viburnums in isolated outbreaks. Gardens change periodically to accommodate events beyond our control.

In November 2002, English Heritage published *The State of the Historic Environment*, the first-ever national audit of all aspects of our

The family of writer A. P. Herbert, assembled in his Hammersmith garden in 1931, on a fashionable crazy-paving terrace by the Thames.

heritage, embracing listed buildings, rural landscapes, ancient monuments and archaeology as well as parks and gardens. Its conclusions were predictable: that the irreplaceable historic environment is under persistent attack from a variety of sources. In 2001, for example, 57 per cent of Grade I and II* listed historic parks and gardens were involved in planning applications, a figure which was noted as being much higher than for any other type of designated asset.

When English Heritage first published its *Register of Parks and Gardens of Special Historic Interest in England* in 1988, around 1,000 sites were identified as nationally important. Recent updates have increased that number to over 1,500. Today's register contains a variety of sites, including cemeteries, hospital grounds and some allotments, though the majority are privately owned gardens or parkland relating to a dwelling or former dwelling. In addition, there are believed to be around 6,000 further sites of local importance that make a considerable contribution to the historic landscape at regional and local level, even though they are not included on the register.

Should we resist the ephemeral nature of these gardens and try to turn back the clock? Sometimes, but with caution. Restorations are undoubtedly useful in helping us to get a better understanding of eminent people for whom their gardens were a significant part of their life – such as Gilbert White at Selborne, Charles Darwin at Down House and William Morris at Red House. And it is instructive as well as entertaining to see a magnificent restoration on the scale of Hampton Court's formerly lost Privy Garden, or the National Trust's resuscitation of the eccentric and exotic Biddulph Grange in Staffordshire. Historic landscapes and large-scale restorations, such as Heligan in Cornwall, do help to bring the past to life and serve an important educational and recreational role.

Yet the fact remains that we can never see these gardens in the precise context in which they were created, any more than a television costume drama can deliver to us the age of Jane Austen. None of us arrives at gardens on horseback or in a *calèche* through treacherous lanes pitted with craters and mud. And the sounds we hear in them are not the swish of the scythe and gentlemanly snip of hand shears, but the petrol roar of strimmers and mowers, perhaps the rumblings of a main road beyond the boundary, or, indeed, the trilling of the mobile telephone. The garden that has evolved over a

Prettily wrought iron on the stairway entrance to Highhead Castle, Cumberland. Plans to renovate have not come to fruition since fire ruined the house in 1956.

hundred years into something completely different is not necessarily of lesser interest, even if, compared with its earlier incarnations, it appears 'lost'. The horticultural marvel of a hundred years ago may now, like Ashton Wold and Warley Place, be an unmanicured haven for wildlife and therefore play a substantially different, yet most valuable role.

The pictures within this book are haunting because they are authentic: moments captured of gardens in their prime, inhabited by people whose lives were very different from ours today. The landscape architect Sir Geoffrey Jellicoe was acutely aware that the gardens he made were transient things, but he was typically philosophical; the fact that the creative idea had surfaced was the important factor. We must go on allowing new creativity to surface, and we must create new gardens of our own time. It is essential that we embrace the present and future, while celebrating, recording and, where it is warranted, preserving the best of the past.

ONE

SOUTH WEST

The simple pleasures of the country garden pervade the lost gardens of the South West, unsullied by the encroachments of the Industrial Revolution. Topiary, traditionally the craft of the cottage gardener, was charmingly celebrated at Compton End (*left*), and in a more sophisticated composition amid the pleasure grounds of Lindridge (*below*). Topiary was important in other gardens of the region, too, forming green architecture at Brockenhurst Park and Tortworth Court, with their sculpted hedges, and at St Catherine's Court, with its signature spires of yew. Steeply sloping ground is a feature in many parts of the South West, providing the potential for dramatic terraces, notably at Cowley Manor and Streatham Hall, where stonework had a strong presence, while the terracing of St Catherine's Court was given a softer, country feel with extensive use of turf.

COWLEY MANOR, GLOUCESTERSHIRE

Although Cowley's manor house still stands and indeed has
undergone significant modernisation – it reopened recently as a chic
hotel with ultra-modern décor – its crisply terraced Victorian
gardens belonged to another age.

It is said that seven springs rise at Cowley, feeding into the River
Churn that runs through the grounds on its determined way over
the Cotswolds to join the River Thames further east. And, being
such a well-watered place, 800 feet above sea level, Cowley has a
long history, certainly dating back to the days of the Norman
Conquest and the Berkeley family, who were for centuries a powerful force in the region. At some stage, the manor of Cowley was
given to Pershore Abbey. An entry for Cowley in the Domesday
Book (1086) states: 'In the demesne are two plough teams and 14
villeins and one bordar [small-holder] with 7 plough-teams. There
are 5 slaves and a mill of 50 pence [annual value] and 6 acres of
meadow and a wood 3 furlongs long by one broad. It is worth 100
shillings [per annum].'

Under the Dissolution of the Monasteries, Henry VIII
endowed Cowley to Westminster Abbey and thereafter a series of
private tenancies followed. The lovely hilltop situation, with its
south-facing slope leading into the valley, must have made it an
irresistible place to build a good house and landscape a fine park.
Henry Brett built the first house of note on the site, in 1674,
placing it close to the church, which still stands in the grounds.
A description from a 1782 survey notes 'an exceeding good Manor-
house, with Outhouses, Stables and a Coach-house all in good
repair and a large Garden. … Close to the steps is a fine sweep for
Carriages. It is situated upon a delightful eminence, and in as good
air as any in England, with a good Terrace before it …'. The survey
also noted a substantial pond of water in the valley, 'which is
constantly supplied with springs arising in it or close to it …'.

Brett, alas, did not manage to enjoy the 'house of note' to the end
of his days, for his fortune was drained away in pursuit of a passion
for bell-ringing – he toured the country at great expense with a
company of ringers. Subsequently, the house changed hands
regularly until, in the mid-nineteenth century, the freehold was
sold by the dean and chapter of Westminster to James Hutchinson,
a man of considerable wealth. Hutchinson built a new house on the
hill in 1850, using the stones of Brett's mansion in its foundations.
He also laid out the garden terraces and a magnificent water
cascade, and created an avenue clearing through the wood on the
opposite hill, aligned along a vista running up to the centre of his
house. (Subsequent alterations under later ownerships mean that
the alignment is no longer central.)

A subsequent owner, Mr (later, Sir) James Horlick, employed
the architect R. A. Briggs to make significant alterations and exten-
sions to Hutchinson's house and its outbuildings, around the close

*Stone terraces and a prodigious amount of statuary ornamented the south-facing
hill below a new house, built in 1850.*

of the nineteenth century. Horlick, a Gloucestershire man hailing from the Forest of Dean, was the son of a saddler. After qualifying as a chemist, he had made his fortune out of Horlicks, the malted beverage, which he patented in America in 1873 in partnership with his brother, William. It had been impossible in the first instance to raise capital to manufacture and market the drink in London, but he returned to his homeland with all his fortune before him, a good portion of which was lavished on the alluring manor of Cowley.

When *Country Life* featured Cowley in August 1906, it noted that 'Mr James Horlick has rounded off the park and pleasure grounds by purchase, chiefly, and has planted, it is locally reported, some 700,000 trees – forest oaks and beeches in the park and by the water's edge, as well as arbutus, various laurels, yews, and other shrubs on the walks and by the fountains.' And, since he had the means to maintain them, the fantastical Baroque conceit of the water gardens, and the statue-filled terraces, with their potted evergreens and neatly bedded-out flowers, were thus captured in their prime – and just in time. Their Victorian imagery looked distinctly old-fashioned when compared with the exuberant

informality being enthusiastically embraced through the Edwardian age. Lutyens and Jekyll were already *à la mode*, with their rustic pavings and romanticised evocations of cottage-garden borders.

Horlick died in 1921 and the property underwent several changes of ownership through the rest of the twentieth century. In 1946, the house (with its manorial rights) was purchased by Gloucestershire County Council as a venue for adult education and youth projects. From 1992 it was used as a residential nursing home and community-care centre. The Victorian gardens had gone, but some new planting was carried out by plantsman-designer Noel Kingsbury, using hardy perennials in the naturalistic 'European' style.

Following a further sale in 1999, Cowley Manor underwent another transformation, this time into a luxury hotel. The silted-up lakes have been dredged and the fountains recently put back into working order, but there are no plans to restore the elaborate terraces.

Above and right: Seven natural springs rise at Cowley, feeding the River Churn and the Manor's serene lake. James Hutchinson's Italianate gardens, created in the 1850s, included this magnificent water cascade.

BROCKENHURST PARK, HAMPSHIRE

When Brockenhurst Park was first photographed for *Country Life*, for two features on 23 and 30 November 1901, the garden was already mature, displaying extensive masonry in its stairways and terraces, surrounded by luxuriant walls of crisply topiarised bay, holm oak, yew and hornbeam. Perhaps more than any other English garden of the time, these rigorously formal grounds captured the essence of an Italian Renaissance garden and, more particularly, its predecessors of Classical Rome. The long canal, enclosed by arcaded topiary, statues and regularly placed potted trees, inspires thoughts of the Emperor Hadrian's ancient villa and its *Canopus*, near Tivoli.

Yet Brockenhurst, the 'wood of the badger', was created in the heart of the New Forest – in an ancient landscape of shady English oaks, Scots pine and heathland pastures, rather than among the scattered umbrella pines and travertine quarries of Latium. William

Gilpin (1724–1804), pioneer of the Picturesque aesthetic and uncle of the garden designer William Sawrey Gilpin, was the vicar of the neighbouring parish of Boldre. He considered the Brockenhurst area to be the most alluring woodland to be found anywhere, its oaks having 'a character peculiar to themselves; they seldom rise into lofty stems as oaks usually do in richer soil, but their branches, which are more adapted to what shipbuilders call knees and elbows, are commonly twisted into the most picturesque forms'.

The formal garden was created for the Morant family as a civilised environment for cultured people, sheltered by its walls and hedges from the cruder landscape of a forest roamed by wild ponies, pigs and deer. It was also a garden almost without flowers, relying for its effect on the varying greens of foliage, both clipped and free-form. The layout can be seen divided into several open courts, separated by formally hedged corridors in the architectural manner as prescribed by Reginald Blomfield.

Although Brockenhurst's inception predates Blomfield's *The Formal Garden in England* (1892) by at least two decades, it could almost be a template for the genre: 'The formal garden, with its insistence on strong bounding lines, is strictly speaking, the only

Above: The Emperor's Court, with its Classical busts set into the niches of the clipped hedges.

Left: Formal hedges frame the west entrance to the Emperor's Court. Each precisely measured vista concluded with a sculpture in the Classical style.

"garden" possible,' declared Blomfield, who would certainly have admired so much green architecture and symmetry. Brockenhurst's long, gravelled walks, enclosed either by neat hedges or by avenues of columnar yews, always led to a focal point – a piece of statuary, a courtyard, or a gateway – which invited further exploration. From the south elevation of the house the canal can be seen, thick with water lilies. It leads to the Emperor's Stairway and from there to the stage set of the Emperor's Court, with its busts on pedestals set into niches in the hedge. The Emperor's Retreat was defined by yew hedges, clipped at the top into rows of ball finials. The Emperor's Guard was a gravelled parterre, surrounded by neat lollipops of trees; clipped ivy and laurel were used elsewhere.

From the many pictures that were taken for *Country Life*, it is clear that this was a gentleman's garden *par excellence*: note the obsession with rectilinear form; the precision-cut topiary; the constant allusions to an Emperor (not Empress, mind, though Victoria was still presiding over vast areas of the world when this garden was made). Note also the arrangements of Imperial personages in cold white marble, and the absence of flowers.

Some of the Brockenhurst views suggest that it could have inspired a variety of later gardens. Close by, at Rhinefield, a not dissimilar canal, with hedged rooms and topiary beyond, was laid out for Mabel Zoe Walker and her husband by architect W. H. Romaine-Walker, to accompany a faux-Elizabethan mansion he had built for them in 1888–91. It could be argued that there are hints of Brockenhurst in Major Lawrence Johnston's garden at Hidcote Manor, Gloucestershire, begun in the years preceding the First World War, although Hidcote is a much more floral affair. The grounds of Anglesey Abbey in Cambridgeshire, largely laid out in the 1930s by the 1st Lord Fairhaven, convey similar sentiments.

The *Country Life* features of November 1901 were full of praise for the maker of the Brockenhurst Park gardens, yet they did not disclose his or her name. An anonymous reader stepped in to set the record straight immediately, writing to the editor: 'I think it only fair to the memory of an old friend to say that they were entirely the creation of the late Mr John Morant, a man of great and discriminating taste and knowledge. Many of the yew hedges and trees which give the gardens such a venerable appearance were actually planted within the last thirty years by him.'

Mr Morant's turreted Victorian château, which replaced an earlier house, was demolished in 1960, since both it and the desperately labour-intensive garden had long run to seed. A smaller, modern house was built in its place, and from the 1960s the Berry family attempted to restore parts of the garden. Though the canal survives, the formal areas have been greatly simplified, and the park, which lost some of its most magnificent trees in the great storm of 1987, is now run as a nature reserve by the Hampshire Wildlife Trust.

The stone-edged canal, with its arrangements of topiaries focused on a Victorian château, which was demolished and replaced by a modern house in 1960.

LINDRIDGE, DEVON

Scenic Lindridge, hidden away down Devon's narrow, high-banked lanes, was always renowned for its trees. Many of them still ornament the park, although the fine seventeenth-century house has gone and its lavish gardens, laid out for Lord Cable just before the First World War, are greatly diminished, having lost their focal point.

Opinion has long been divided as to whether the origins of the name 'Lindridge' spring from local geology – a ridge of limestone – or from local woodlands, including the Old English linden, or lime, tree. At any rate, at the close of the eighteenth century, the historian Revd Richard Polwhele noted 'a beautiful hanging wood' and 'the woods cloathing the hills, or waving in dark masses of shadow from the chasms of the limerock; and the gay diversities of green exhibited in rich distinctness by the oak, the beech, the elm, the fir, the lime, the chestnut, the plane, and the walnut – all flourishing with uncommon vigor ...'. It is certainly a rare location, sloping gently down to the south and west, with far-reaching westward views of the high tors of Dartmoor.

Later, Lindridge became famous for the luxuriant growth of its cedars; when Christopher Hussey visited in 1938, he found 'the cedars are the first things in the landscape to strike the eye whether in approaching the house or looking outwards from it'.

The gardens in the immediate vicinity of the house were initiated by James Ransome, in consultation with the Veitch Nursery of Exeter in 1913, but the grand plan was finally settled and the planting arranged by architect Edward White, of Milner, White and Son, and completed in 1913–14. White's scheme included a new terraced garden descending the slope from the south elevation of the house. Its formal, symmetrical arrangement of flowerbeds and flagstone paths, enclosed by a balustrade, led to a lower tier of lawns and topiaries. The unmortared joints of its central path were planted in the style of the day with low creepers, the whole leading to a rotunda, centrally placed within a lily pool and enclosed by yew hedges.

Christopher Hussey observed that the layout was beautifully planned, yet lacked strength when looked down upon from the

Above: *The entry to the Italian Garden from the lawns. The mortar joints of the two stone piers were picked out with carefully trained ivy.*

Right: *The original view was centred upon the house, which burnt down in 1963. The elegant eight-columned rotunda has been replaced by a smaller, inferior model, though the pool remains intact.*

house. 'The general effect inclines to be spotty and the architectural features insufficiently bold in relation to the extent and dignity of the plan.' An interesting use of ivy was recorded on a pair of stone piers near the rotunda, where the climber was pruned and trained to just cover the mortar joints, giving an exaggerated 'brickwork' effect that must have been very laborious to maintain.

On the slope above the house, to the north-west, a pergola walk of stone piers and stout oak crossbeams led to steps descending to sculpted lawns ornamented by wonderful trees and a rectangular pond. One charming photograph of it suggests that its inspiration could have been a late-seventeenth- or early-eighteenth-century canal, such as survives at Hall Barn, Buckinghamshire, centred upon a Classical 'temple'. However, this serene stretch of water was in fact an Olympic-sized swimming pool, though one designed to fit seamlessly into its Classically inspired location. Hussey's article noted that 'since the photograph was taken the little Temple at the far end, and the screen of bushes have been removed, revealing the great view over rolling fields to Dartmoor'.

What became of splendid Lindridge? The house tragically burnt down in the early 1960s and thus began the undoing of the garden. Nothing came of various proposals for new development over the succeeding decades until permission was granted for new housing in the vicinity of the old house in the mid-1990s.

Today, the 23 acres of gardens and paddocks surround a closely knit development of twenty-one houses. Some of the great trees must have been felled in the course of building, though many others had most likely fallen in earlier storms. Of the celebrated cedars, only two survive and these, alas, are not remarkable specimens of the genus. And, of course, by the late twentieth century, Lindridge's mighty elms, which had been arranged so protectively around the house, had succumbed to Dutch Elm disease.

Meanwhile, the terraced gardens and the walk to the rotunda are remarkably intact; although the planting has been simplified, yet it is pretty and appropriate, with pink roses, nepeta and lady's mantle. However, many key features and embellishments have simply disappeared. The handsome rotunda has been replaced by a smaller, off-the-shelf version, which, having only six columns, does not line up properly with its access paths. Even more sadly, all but a minuscule section of the Olympic pool has been filled in, topped by a poorly designed and executed rose garden. If the pool's temple had disappeared by October 1938, it, or one like it, has returned, though the present temple has been turned into an undignified changing room for the truncated pool, the space behind its four columns filled in with doors and windows and hung with a jaunty lifebelt. These poorly executed substitutes have been officially listed, and the residents of what is now called Lindridge Park have been unable so far to reinstate the dignified garden features which have been so crudely altered.

Resembling an elegant canal, the Olympic-sized swimming pool was framed by Lindridge's great elms and cedars. It was a landscaping masterpiece.

TORTWORTH COURT, GLOUCESTERSHIRE

When *Country Life* first featured Tortworth, in 1899, it was the seat of the 3rd Earl of Ducie, Lord Lieutenant of Gloucestershire and one of the nation's foremost dendrologists. When these photographs were taken, Lord Ducie had already been planting trees on his vast and scenic estate for some forty-five years; he was just twenty-five years old when he inherited in 1853.

He also inherited a new mansion, which replaced one built by earlier owners, the Throckmortons. For a Victorian tree enthusiast, Tortworth, with its fertile soil, extensive wooded hills and soft lawns sloping down to a serpentine lake, provided the perfect setting in which to plant a gentleman's arboretum. Here Lord Ducie could carefully compose a series of pictures with hundreds of saplings – all the most coveted new species grown from seeds sent by plant-hunters in far-flung lands. His collection included dozens of the rarest species of oaks, scores of acers, and countless North American and Asian conifers and much else, organised into compositions of contrasting form and foliage colour. Many specimens were regarded as the finest to be seen anywhere in Europe.

Tortworth's most famous tree long predates the Ducie family, however. The Tortworth Chestnut is a huge, spreading specimen

resembling a small copse. Legend has it that it grew from a nut planted before the Norman Conquest, and written accounts of its magnitude go back to the twelfth century. Lord Ducie's passion for trees continued for the rest of his long life – he died on 27 October 1921, in his ninety-fifth year.

The formal gardens of knife-edged and topiarised hedges, circular beds of sub-tropical flowers, and punctuation marks of Irish yew gradually disappeared in the twentieth century. The estate was split up and most of the arboretum now belongs to Leyhill Prison, with the lake unceremoniously separated from the gardens by chain-link fencing. The Victorian mansion has undergone conversion into a 189-room business hotel, its 30-acre gardens winding around complexes of new bedrooms and car parking. The circular flowerbeds have been re-established in a simplified pattern, but Lord Ducie's extensive kitchen gardens and nurseries are long gone, though his splendid conservatory has been rescued from dereliction and turned into a restaurant.

Right: *The formal gardens and topiary hedges beside the house. The entrance gate beyond bears the legend 'WELCOME' in carved stone on its outer face.*

Below: *The view from the house in 1899. In Lord Ducie's day, the landscape read as a complete scene, with his magnificent trees framing the serpentine lake.*

ST CATHERINE'S COURT, SOMERSET

In its early years, *Country Life* was so inspired by St Catherine's Court that it featured the property several times within a short period. It is not surprising, for the Tudor manor house, sympathetically extended in 1915, sits halfway up the side of an exquisitely peaceful valley and still enjoys pastoral views of little hills and patchwork fields – no ugliness intrudes on the bucolic scene.

The first article appeared on 24 December 1898, shortly after the death of the then owner, the Hon. Mrs Charlotte Olivia Drummond. The late Mrs Drummond had lived to an extremely old age (she was born a hundred years before, in 1798) and therefore her garden was laid out to mid-nineteenth-century taste and was not up-to-date in its planting. Yet its grand stairways, with stone steps, balustrades and crisply levelled terraces, made sense of the steeply sloping site. However, by 1898, a 'quaintness of design' was noted, and the gardens were praised for combining strictly formal planting with 'the freely natural'.

Gertrude Jekyll found her way to St Catherine's Court not long afterwards, and supplied *Country Life* with two more articles on the property, published in December 1906. Characteristically, she sounded at times like the stern teacher reprimanding a gifted child who could do better. It seems that the intervening years had yielded little progress in bringing the gardens in line with twentieth-century style, so there poured forth from Miss Jekyll a lecture on what ought to be seen at St Catherine's Court, rather than what the pictures indicate was actually there. 'In a place like this, gardening is easy … but it should be done just rightly, for there are numberless ways of going wrong,' she wrote, though she was first careful to highlight all its good points – the excellence of the hard landscaping and its noble Italian style. 'Never smother the wall terraces with ivy or ampelopsis,' she carried on, no doubt observing that these plants engulf many of the walls in the photographs.

Instead, she suggested planting clematis in modest colours of varied lilacs to clothe the walls, 'and even through and over the carved balustrade' (which had been photographed in its stony nakedness). However, the curious mix of styles already noted in 1898 suggests that the garden was at a transitional stage: Jekyll's favoured lavenders, delphiniums and peonies – all ideal plants for the alkaline soil – were there, but they existed cheek by jowl with the Victorian legacy of oddly shaped beds cut out of the lawns, and clipped blobs of undistinguished evergreenery.

These Jekyll articles bring out magnificently all her horticultural hobby-horses: the rightness of old-fashioned roses; the need for a garden to set aside an area for Michaelmas daisies; her preoccupation with poking plants into crevices – 'the little plant looking as if it had come there by some chance'. Irish yews, which have naturally columnar growth, had been planted at St Catherine's in various places and 'trimmed to a shape', she observed, before

A signature pair of yews echo the church tower. Viewed from the terrace, the parterre resembled a 'quaint' flower garden, laid out on rising ground.

scolding: 'Whether it is ever desirable to clip Irish yews is very doubtful. They will only clip into one form, and that is not a graceful one.' The humiliation was not yet over. Sprouts of pampas grass and, particularly, assorted specimen conifers had been planted about the lawns on all sides. She then delivered her *coup de grâce*. 'The quiet lawns of these old places should be jealously guarded, especially from the intrusion of specimen conifers … whose presence has destroyed the character of many a fine old garden. Happily, we know better now, and the vandalisms of the last generation are no longer practised.'

Ironically, a century on, St Catherine's Court's gardens appear closer in spirit to the Jekyll ideal of romantic antiquity. Much of the Victoriana has been swept away in favour of uninterrupted lawns, although columnar cypress trees have replaced many of the Irish yews. Self-sown toadflax, valerian and corydalis spring from mortar joints in the walls. Several yew topiaries have survived, but two massive yew cones near the house, formerly kept level with the chimneys, have been cut back to less than half that height and turned into more manageable flat-topped drums. Planting is in soft colours, with many pink roses, ceanothus, lavenders and lady's

mantle. All of the masonry survives, though a Palladian-style stairway, not in keeping with the style or quality of the property, has been added to the south front at some stage.

The current garden also has a wildness which is not without charm: the old kitchen garden has been taken over by knee-high grass colonised by wild orchids; a formerly crisp hedge has grown out into a row of fat yew trees casting deep shade over what used to be a bowling green on the steep western hillside.

Photographs of Victorian turf stairways are very rare, but one was taken at St Catherine's Court, charmingly styled with the gardener standing in the distance pointing towards a monkey-puzzle tree. That tree has gone and in its place resides a large *Thuja plicata*; the shallow risers of turf have been smoothed into a plain lawn, although it slopes up the hill in three obvious undulations suggestive of the old pattern. But the setting, beside an ancient church, is as bewitching as ever.

Above: *The turf stairway. The parterre was behind the high wall on the right; further up the hill lay the kitchen garden, beyond the monkey-puzzle tree.*

Right: *Terracing the ground made sense of the steeply sloping site, although the many beds cut out of the lawns created a somewhat busy scene.*

STREATHAM HALL, DEVON

On the north-west side of Exeter city, the ancient manor of Duryard was originally a wooded hunting park. King Athelstan gifted the manor to Exeter in the tenth century, and a Domesday Book entry shows that 960 acres of Duryard were cultivated by the citizens of Exeter, the great woods providing timber for building the city. In 1866, a house known as Duryard Lodge, along with surrounding hilly land that was part of the original Duryard Estate, was sold to Richard Thornton West, a merchant with the East India Company. Having what in those days amounted to a colossal fortune (he inherited over a million pounds from his uncle, Richard Thornton, who is said to have made his money by blockade running in the Napoleonic Wars), Thornton West demolished Duryard Lodge and built himself Streatham Hall, in the terraced and balustraded Italianate style much in vogue since Charles Barry's success at Trentham and, more particularly, at Shrubland Park.

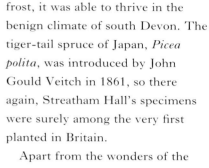

The sloping site of Streatham Hall suited the Italian mode, with its stone stairways and terraced walks, punctuated at appropriate junctions with elegant statuary. Mr Thornton West employed the famous Exeter nursery-men Messrs Veitch to plant the grounds with the very latest and rarest exotic trees and shrubs. They were well placed to do so, since Veitch had made their name by sending out plant collectors, including the brothers William and Thomas Lobb, John Gould Veitch and, subsequently, the great Ernest Wilson, to distant lands in search of hitherto unknown species.

The 1899 *Country Life* feature noted a 'very wide avenue' beyond massive gates at the entrance 'charmed with the broad sweeps of grass, the green slopes, and many conifers, as well as a host of flowering trees, which seem to revel in the place'. This carriage drive appears to have followed the footprint of the original route to Duryard Lodge, though it was the Veitches who planted matched pairs of trees, *Cupressus lawsoniana* and *Thujopsis borealis*, along its length. Within the terraced gardens the correspondent recorded 'fine hollies and conifers in particular ... [plus] flower vases, with beautiful examples of *Retinospora plumosa*, golden yew, and other beautiful things'.

Above: *The Veitch Nursery was employed to plant the grounds with the latest tree and shrub species being sent to England by intrepid plant-hunters.*

Left: *The vast palm house was one of the finest in the west of England, packed with arrangements of tender ferns and palms.*

Although no records have survived of the transactions between Veitch Nurseries and Richard Thornton West, the trees, as they grew, spoke for themselves. Streatham Hall received some of the earliest examples of *Chamaecyparis lawsoniana* and *Tsuga mertensiana*, the mountain hemlock, two of the conifers that arrived from the western seaboard of North America in 1854; although Lawson's cypress is commonplace today, it was a great novelty when Streatham Hall was in its infancy. *Thujopsis dolabrata* was introduced from Japan in 1853, and, also in 1853, the bristle-cone or Santa Lucia fir, *Abies bracteata*, came to Britain. A native of the Santa Lucia mountains of California and not completely resistant to frost, it was able to thrive in the benign climate of south Devon. The tiger-tail spruce of Japan, *Picea polita*, was introduced by John Gould Veitch in 1861, so there again, Streatham Hall's specimens were surely among the very first planted in Britain.

Apart from the wonders of the arboretum, the conservatory and palm house were selected for special praise in *Country Life*: 'The palm house at Streatham Hall is certainly one of the finest in the West of England, and is artistically planted with ferns, palms, and foliage plants, tastefully disposed amongst the rockwork. The house is 71 feet long and 40 feet wide, and is a cool and pleasant retreat in which may be seen many noble palms.'

Richard Thornton West's widow was chatelaine of Streatham Hall at the time of the *Country Life* feature, but after the rather early death of their son, Richard Bowerman West, in 1901, the estate went rapidly downhill. It was acquired in a 'near derelict' state in 1922 by a college which later became the University of Exeter.

Today, Streatham Hall still stands, but is known as Reed Hall and is a major part of the university's campus. Large sections of the grounds have been overtaken by the various faculty buildings, by sports areas and other infrastructure characteristic of university life. The great glasshouses are long gone, and where the grounds are still tended, they are much simplified. However, the university has been aware of its great horticultural inheritance at Streatham Hall and has continued to build up the impressive plant collections. While it is clear that many of Thornton West's trees have already reached the end of their natural life, others of the original Veitch plantings continue to thrive and the campus is regarded as probably the most scenic in the country. It is certainly of great botanical importance and is regularly opened to visitors.

KELWAYS NURSERY, SOMERSET

When *Country Life* featured Kelways in 1898, the nursery was at the zenith of its success. Founded in 1851, it prospered with the rise of industrial wealth and the expansion of the middle classes, supplying herbaceous plants to the masses from its extensive fields. By the end of the nineteenth century, it was the biggest general nursery in the country and possibly the world. Kelways at this time owned several hundred acres around Langport, and its hefty catalogues of the *fin de siècle* period, each loftily entitled *Manual of Horticulture*, were peppered with photographs of 'Kelway Borders' – mixed herbaceous plants – on glorious display at a number of country homes. You could also buy 'Kelway Pæony Borders' – 'a very handsome addition to a garden of any size,' declared the 1909 catalogue. '"Pæony" is almost a synonym for Kelway,' gushed *The Onlooker* magazine. 'Many a pilgrimage to Langport is made by visiting Americans; they go to see the latest creations evolved by the genius of the place … they give themselves up to the witchery of pæony perfume, and closing their eyes, see moonlight and dark red roses, and hear nightingales singing of delicious misery – and, being thus wrought upon, they order numberless roots to be sent across the water.' At Pæony Valley – a Kelways field beside a railway track – the London to Plymouth train used to stop in the season for people to get out and admire the surroundings.

Kelways specialised in about seventy different gaillardias and similar quantities of pyrethrums (now classified as *Tanacetum*) – plants which are not widely admired today; 30 acres were devoted to gladioli, while irises and delphiniums were also bred in great variety. *Country Life*'s photographer visited at gladiolus time, recording the flowers being harvested and packed for the flower markets of London. The article noted that Mr James Kelway, 'still hale at eighty-three, is one of the greatest authorities upon gladiolus culture, and we well remember his interesting paper upon the flower read before the Royal Horticultural Society in the autumn of 1890. … he had cultivated the gladiolus for sixty years, from the time that *G. psittacinus* was first introduced into this country.' It was the success that Kelways had with creating new gladiolus hybrids which apparently led to its breeding programmes for gaillardia and pyrethrum.

Mighty Kelways went bust in 1930, a victim of seed-crop failures and changed attitudes after the First World War – houses no longer had large teams of gardeners to tend labour-intensive acres. After a reprieve in 1948, when new owners invigorated the site with a hybridisation programme for bearded irises, the nursery underwent mixed fortunes in the 1980s and early 1990s. Now it has settled again in new ownership and new, scaled-down premises not far from its original nursery. A programme is under way to re-establish its prominence as a leading grower of the peonies and irises for which it was once so famous.

Flower harvests at the nation's biggest nursery in 1898. Gaillardias, pyrethrums and gladioli were specialities, as well as peonies and Kelways' famous irises.

COMPTON END, HAMPSHIRE

Compton End is one of the most appealing small gardens in the *Country Life* archives. It is also one of the best recorded. It first appeared on 15 December 1900, in a feature entitled 'New Homes in Old Houses'. This was a popular theme of the time, focusing on old country cottages and farmhouses 'suitable for summer homes for people with country tastes, but whose business lay in town' – predating today's preoccupation with rural idyll 'makeovers'.

In the late 1890s, Compton End had been bought by an architect, G. H. Kitchin, who worked in the Arts and Crafts style from offices in nearby Winchester. The 1900 article described how he was restoring and extending the former farmhouse, which had for some while been split up into two labourers' cottages. It also showed Kitchin's plan of both the house and its garden – at that time, the cottage was still surrounded almost entirely by fruit and vegetable plots, with a traditional farmyard complete with thatched barns and a duckpond occupying the northern corner. The published photographs of 1900 showed Kitchin's first ventures in the garden – a springtime view of the narrow Sundial Path leading from the house front, flanked by narrow lawns, and long borders filled with pheasant's-eye narcissi. A return to the same view a few

months later shows the lawns edged with pinks, the borders burgeoning with delphiniums and verbascum, and the owner (one assumes) standing at the doorway patting his dog.

George Kitchin himself wrote the second article, published on 23 August 1919, and again supplied a plan. This later one demonstrates how dramatically he had tamed the plot over the intervening years into a disciplined Edwardian acre of hedged rooms and symmetrically ordered flower borders (with both paved and grass paths between); he had also created a wild-garden-with-rockery, laid out along the south-western boundary.

Kitchin inherited 'some fine old yew trees and clipped boxes', which, he noted – thanks to the shears of a shepherd who had lived there many years – promised to help in the making of the garden. By 1919, the topiaries had grown into mature cottage-garden peacocks and new paths between beds were lined with box balls and saxifrages. One of the old but untamed yew trees had flourished in

Above: *The old entrance from the lane. G. H. Kitchin later remodelled it to provide more privacy, so callers could not wander straight into the gardens.*

Right: *A view from the south-west. The stone steps led up from the wild garden along a vista to the glazed garden room.*

the middle of the garden, but darkened the cottage windows so much that it 'was taken ruthlessly in hand some twelve years ago; its head was chopped off, the side boughs were fastened down, and, after three or four years as a scarecrow, it greened up and filled out,' reported Kitchin. From the photographs we can see that the tree pleasingly echoed the rounded contours of the thatched cottage roof, though Kitchin described it as being 'in the form of an Arab mosque or marabout … with arbours within, one facing north and the other south'.

Beyond the yew arbour he laid out a Pond Garden, with grass paths leading between L-shaped flowerbeds, the whole enclosing a square-shaped lily pool. 'This plot of ground fell so much towards the south that it did not lend itself to formal gardening, which is a thing to be avoided on a slope,' he advised. And so it remained for some years as an unresolved place, in the short term to be used for bush fruit and a nursery ground. Later, the conundrum was solved

Above: *The levelled-out Pond Garden, with its downland views through the arched branches of an ancient, storm-battered yew tree.*

Left: *The garden room was a suntrap, glazed on two sides and used year-round, the doors always open. The steps led up to Kitchin's bedroom and terrace.*

by excavating a deep pond to form the middle feature. Its spoil went a long way to providing the necessary material for levelling out this part of the site.

According to Kitchin: 'The chaos was considerable, for the soil is deep loam on chalk, and the good earth of the lower portion of the plot had first to be removed into a heap to make room to bury the chalk from the bottom of the pond, and then it and the top soil from the pond had to be laid on the chalk to form the new surface.' This area was ultimately declared a most successful part of the garden. Kitchin built 12-inch-wide stone edgings around the surrounding beds to solve the problems of die-back on the turf where exuberant plants flop over, and also helping to 'emphasise the design in a pleasing manner'. The beds were planted with bush roses and scarlet phlox, with tall tulips to light up the spring.

One of Kitchin's charming earlier additions to the house was a tile-paved, sun-filled garden room with one glazed wall facing south-east; the other, with glazed double doors, opened to the south-west. It was constantly used, and had the advantage of a flat lead roof, which, catching rainwater and also the morning sun, formed 'a delightful open-air bathroom', reached from a doorway made in the wall of the adjacent bedroom. From the glazed garden room, which was used for meals year-round with the doors flung open, a paved path was laid between square flowerbeds (the corner of each bed marked by a box ball), eventually leading down steps into the wild garden.

Later, Kitchin altered the opposite side of the garden to create a new porch and hallway of oak beams and brickwork on the house end facing directly on to the lane, where mains electricity and water could at last be accessed. A smart pedestrian entrance was created and the garden screened off from casual view. 'Before this, what is now the garden porch had been the front door, and, being a favourite place for tea and outdoor meals in the summer, it was impossible to escape callers and say "not at home" when caught in the act,' he admitted.

A hundred-year-old photograph of the farmyard adjacent to the new entrance reveals a rural ensemble that was even then beginning to disappear from the British countryside. Here you could find a cluster of barns and byres under moss-covered, low-sweeping thatch, with a dew-pond in one corner by the lane. A fence of rustic palings separated the house and its adjoining woodshed from the yard; beyond the back door, a little path led to the potting shed and greenhouse.

At the time when Kitchin acquired the property it was known as the Old Rectory – a name that seems rather grand for this little house, but, as the 1900 feature suggested, 'possibly it was so at one time, for rectories were usually modest affairs before the rise of corn prices in the great [Napoleonic] war'. Yet its position, a long way from the church, more naturally suggested it was a secondary farm on the estate, scenically positioned at the head of one of the branch valleys of the River Itchen, 'with downs behind and fields in front'. Kitchin noted that it had been built on an ancient thoroughfare dating back to Roman times, a conjecture reinforced by the discovery of Roman coins lurking in the garden soil. The ground also yielded other treasures, such as Jacobean and even Turkish coins, and Cromwellian tobacco pipes.

Though the cottage was ancient, as a humble building its history is not well documented. However, local tradition suggests that Compton End played its part in the Civil War, for one of Cromwell's generals was billeted there during the siege of Winchester; certainly, Cromwell's camp and cannons were settled in the hills further up the little lane. In autumn 1645, after several days of attacks on the castle stronghold, the Royalists were defeated.

George Kitchin's family continued to live at Compton End until the early 1990s. Since then, the property has changed hands twice. Kitchin's orchard was sold off as a plot for new houses and the yew arbour and farmyard disappeared long ago. Much of the basic lay-out of the garden can still be discerned, though the planting has altered over the years.

A large old yew tree was ruthlessly cut back and reshaped. Eventually it made a green, tunneled arbour, 'in the form of an Arab mosque or marabout'.

TWO

SOUTH EAST

The lost gardens of the South East encompass the broadest range of styles to be found anywhere in the country. The great variety of Victorian horticultural passions was handsomely displayed in the glasshouses of Cherkley Court, in the parterres and arcades of Muntham Court (*left*), and in the timberwork and evergreen shrubberies of Alma-Tadema's garden in London (*below*).

A widely held enthusiasm for rock gardens, initiated in the second half of the nineteenth century, flowered brilliantly in the early twentieth at Swaylands, and took on a fashionably Japanese accent at Sedgwick Park. In contrast, Shepherd's Gate, a new house built during Edward VII's short reign, represented a brighter, less cluttered order for the twentieth century, while at ancient Valewood Farm we see Gertrude Jekyll's cottage-garden style fused with the new wave of Modernism.

CHERKLEY COURT, SURREY

The course of the River Mole meanders extravagantly through the North Downs, its valley having carved a scenic landscape between Leatherhead and Dorking, which has inspired writers and poets for centuries. Keats, Dryden and Robert Louis Stevenson visited the countryside around Cherkley regularly, while a few novelists, including Richard Brinsley Sheridan and George Meredith, lived locally. Although the Mole's course at this point is now joined by the busy A24 dual carriageway, a century ago it was an area of great peacefulness, famous for its glamorous country houses occupied by influential figures of the Edwardian age.

Cherkley's neighbouring estates included Norbury Park, famous for its 'Druid's Grove' of ancient yews; Denbies (now England's largest wine estate); John Evelyn's former home at Wotton; Deepdene, which had belonged to the art collector Thomas Hope; Polesden Lacey, the home of society hostess Mrs Ronald Greville

Above: *The large water-lily pond, photographed in 1899. Later, in Lord Beaverbrook's time, it was converted into a swimming pool.*

Left: *Double doors from the dining room led into the magnificent conservatory, with its Moorish filigree screen inspiring thoughts of the Alhambra at Granada.*

from 1906; and Sir Edgar Vincent's Esher Place (see pages 80–1), a few meanders further downstream.

When *Country Life* depicted the glories of Cherkley in 1900, it was the home of a retired Birmingham industrialist and philanthropist, Mr Abraham Dixon. The house was then virtually new, since an earlier one had been seriously damaged by fire in 1893, and Mr Dixon had had to rebuild, this time choosing a slightly French Gothic style. From its hilltop position, looking south-west over the Mickleham Valley to Box Hill, it enjoyed magnificent views, with 'the sylvan heights of Norbury full in the prospect'.

From formally laid-out gardens immediately around the house, the ground slipped away in easy sweeps of lawn down to an arboretum displaying, in the Victorian manner, the latest imports of conifers in their varied shapes and multiple manifestations of green, golden or glaucous foliage. Many of them must have struggled, or needed to be cosseted, being planted in the thin and highly alkaline soil of this chalkland district. Beyond the arboretum, a further drop down the hill led to a more natural landscape of native beech, box and yew woodlands. An avenue was created through the grounds providing a long drive between alternating pairs of *Abies pinsapo* and *Cupressus lawsoniana*, which would be regarded as gloomy and overly stylised today, though in the late nineteenth century it was *à la mode*.

Most significant of all at Cherkley were its wonderful glass-houses, erected on level ground immediately beside the house and said to cover an acre of land, though such an extent may have included the productive glass needed for fruit trees and vineries. From the dining room there was access through a broad doorway straight into the conservatory, which was – extravagantly for the day – illuminated by electricity, with plenty of dangling glass lights arranged in varying sizes and colours.

Displays within the great conservatory were in the 'natural' style with planted-up beds crammed with artistic arrangements of tropical dracaenas, assorted cacti, coloured-leaved coleus in great variety, and lilies springing out of forests of adiantum ferns. There were fountains and pools to help maintain humidity and to show off further treasures, such as the exquisite lotus flower, *Nelumbo nucifera*, and its bizarre seedpods. Pelargoniums and begonias would have been planted among the more luxuriant foliage for shots of vivid colour; climbers undoubtedly would have included fragrant jasmines and pale-blue plumbago. One of the conservatory's key features was a Moorish filigree screen inspiring thoughts of the Alhambra and the serene gardens of the Generalife.

Even more exciting was the humid Victoria Regia house, separated from the conservatory by large glazed doors and containing a huge, circular pool that was home to what we now know as *Victoria amazonica* water lilies. Few gardens – then or now – had the space and infrastructure required to nurture these plants to perfection, though they also thrived at Chatsworth and at Kew. The jungle around the pool included palms, papyrus and banana trees. Behind the great conservatory was yet another glasshouse, dedicated to quantities of camellias, and also to both red- and white-flowered forms of lapageria. And beyond the camellias were 'large plants of the guava … which fruits regularly, and other tropical growths'.

Outdoors, beside the house, the Italian garden was splendid, too, having a substantial rectangular pool liberally starred with water lilies. Patterns of mounded-up flowerbeds were cut into the lawn around it, some edged with box, others with bedding – probably alyssum or lobelia – and at least one bed planted with the incongru-ously large-leaved *Gunnera manicata*, upstaging everything else nearby.

In 1909, the thirty-year-old Canadian newspaper baron William Maxwell Aitken (later the 1st Lord Beaverbrook) bought Cherkley Court, doubtless realising its potential for cultivating influential contacts. Rudyard Kipling persuaded him to buy it and the Kiplings advised upon some of the refurbishments. There seem to be no records of when the glasshouses disappeared, but it is likely that they perished during the years leading up to the sale to Aitken. Cherkley hosted many visitors during the fifty years that followed. Guests of the Beaverbrooks included prime ministers – among them fellow Canadian Bonar Law, Herbert Asquith and Winston Churchill, Rudyard Kipling, who composed a poem for the first visitors' book, Duff Cooper, Arnold Bennett and the German ambas-sador, Joachim von Ribbentrop.

At Cherkley, the Beaverbrook empire was efficiently run, with news headlines conjured up on the terraces and barked down the tele-phone to Fleet Street. Financiers 'were charmed and disarmed over dinner; politicians were argued with, and crushed over a weekend'. When the novelist William Gerhardie asked whether Max was an abbreviation for Maximilian, Lord Beaverbrook replied, 'No: Maximultimillion.'

During the Second World War the house was occupied by evacuees, and afterwards it was no longer needed for hosting glittering parties. The gardens were simplified, leaving little trace of their late-Victorian vintage, although the water-lily pool in the Italian garden survives, having at some stage been converted into a swimming pool. Parts of the estate were sold off and built over, though much of the landscape remains intact.

Recently there has been some action at Cherkley. Following protracted debate with the local planners and conservation bodies, both the house and gardens have been extensively refurbished for the Beaverbrook Foundation; the house is to be used in a limited way for corporate functions, weddings and a few public day openings, along the lines of Spencer House in London. The gardens, partially redesigned and partially restored, will be opened to the public during 2004 for the first time in Cherkley's history, though the great glasshouses have gone forever.

Above: *The Victoria Regia house was a remarkable and costly greenhouse devoted to cultivating the difficult and exotic* Victoria amazonica *water lilies.*

Right: *The exquisite lotus flower,* Nelumbo nucifera, *in one of the pools in the steamy conservatory. Its seedpods are as remarkable as its blooms.*

34 GROVE END ROAD, LONDON

The renowned painter Sir Lawrence Alma-Tadema had recently died when *Country Life* featured the garden at his home in St John's Wood, on 23 November 1912. 'The owners of town houses are generally not very enterprising in the treatment of their available garden space, which is often by no means contemptible, particularly in the neighbourhood of Regent's Park,' declared the anonymous author. Although it could never be called a typical London garden, 34 Grove End Road demonstrated some quite splendid woodwork, while its quantity of mature trees, clipped hollies and thickets of evergreen shrubs gave no hint of the urban sprawl nearby.

The plot, including its house, covered three-quarters of an acre of level ground, with pools and flowerbeds cut out of neat lawns and pressed hoggin paths creating a circuit for a leisurely stroll.

Left: *Alma-Tadema created many personal enhancements to his home and garden, including his signature wrought in iron over the covered walkway.*

Below: *One garden feature that initially appealed to the artist was the carved timber colonnade by the pond, complemented by equally luxuriant plants.*

Urns on pedestals were home to leggy geraniums – foolproof plants ideal for city gardens, bearing bright, jolly flowers for a long season. 'With the increasing pleasure which people take in hours spent and meals eaten in the open air, it is good to take stock of the possibilities which lie open to dwellers in London,' the feature advised. 'Miracles of privacy can be wrought by a judicious and generous use of *treillage* and hardy climbing things, where tall walls would mean undue expenditure.' The feature also suggested *trompe l'œil* effects to decorate ugly walls, using trelliswork, to create the impression of 'receding vistas', and arcading.

Much of the garden had already been created before Alma-Tadema acquired what was then No.17 Grove End Road in the early 1880s – a renumbering of the houses in 1901 turned it into No.34. It had been the home of the French painter James Tissot, but was abandoned by him in 1882 after the death of Kathleen Newton, his mistress. Although Alma-Tadema lavishly furnished and enlarged the house, one of the original features that had initially appealed to him was the famous carved timber colonnade of squared Ionic columns and ball finials beside the garden pond; Tissot had included it in a number of his paintings.

Alma-Tadema's enhancements to his home were always his personal creations: he remodelled the doorway after a Roman example he had seen in the newly excavated ruins of Pompeii; the rainspouts were fashioned as lions' heads; and he created a weather vane in the shape of an artist's palette. Ironwork supporting the covered walkway up to the house bore the name Tadema within its pattern. This area, lining the mosaic-tiled path, was a sheltered garden packed with tender plants and fragrant blossoms arranged in a charming muddle of assorted pots, where glimpses of the garden could be caught through the tracery of foliage and flowers.

Alma-Tadema added to the sculptural colonnades and trelliswork begun by Tissot; a study of his paintings immediately demonstrates why such architectural structures appealed greatly to him. Born Laurens Tadema in Friesland, Holland, in 1836, his lifelong interest in history and archaeology as a painter had begun as a student at the Antwerp Academy. His gravitation towards Classical subjects was inflamed by a visit to Italy – and particularly Pompeii – with his first wife. Not long afterwards, on becoming widowed, he moved to London, but memories of Italian pergolas and Pompeiian marble continued to inspire his work. His huge commercial success and prolific output, including society portraits, made him a rich man who was able to lavish improvements on his home and garden and give extravagant, well-attended parties. Needless to say the dress code was frequently fancy, and the artist himself favoured a costume of the Emperor Nero.

Alma-Tadema's genre of painting located him among other Victorian Olympians such as Lord Leighton, Albert Moore and E. J. Poynter. The popularity of their art added fuel to the fire of an Italianate revival in garden design, although it was Harold A. Peto, the architect and landscape gardener, who translated it more seamlessly into the English garden setting. Alma-Tadema is known to have turned his creativity into actual stone elsewhere. In 1909, a pair of large, curved stone seats designed by him was installed at Sandringham, arranged around a Venetian wellhead, with the whole covered by a massive, vine-covered pergola.

Sir Lawrence Alma-Tadema received his knighthood in 1899 and it was followed by an Order of Merit in 1905. His second wife died in 1909 and was buried at Kensal Green Cemetery. Though Sir Lawrence had hoped to be buried beside her, his wish was not fulfilled. He died aged seventy-six at a spa in Wiesbaden and, as one of the most popular painters of his time, was buried in the crypt of St Paul's Cathedral, alongside Leighton, Millais, and Holman Hunt. Not long afterwards, his great house and its contents were sold off and the house was converted into apartments, destroying much of his lavish work. Much of the area suffered bombing during the Second World War and was subsequently rebuilt. A mid-twentieth-century house now occupies the corner site where Alma-Tadema's home once stood.

Alma-Tadema added to the sculptural colonnades and trelliswork begun by Tissot; the architectural element appealed to his love of Classical iconography.

SHEPHERD'S GATE, SUSSEX

Shepherd's Gate, amid the Wealden clays and sandy heaths of Ashdown Forest, was the Edwardian home of Horace Hutchinson, a celebrity in the world of sport at the turn of the twentieth century. It was designed by Maberley Smith, an Arts and Crafts architect who was so pleased with the results that he built a home of similar plan for himself, near Henley.

The house was built in the revivalist style, with gabled roofs, mullioned windows and massive chimney-stacks. In the *Country Life* article published in 1910, the author noted that some of the windows 'suffer from the infliction of plate-glass and in some cases also of valanced wood boxes to hold outside blinds'. He went on to drive the point home: 'Modern architects and clients are apt to forget that, when a new house is built from a design which some-what closely copies an old style, the composition must suffer if essential features of the old style are obliterated or warped, and if

Above: An unpublished photograph of Mrs Hutchinson and family assembled by the porte-cochère; the steps behind led up to the pergola walk.

Left: A simple pergola lined with white lilies was a popular Edwardian conceit, following publication of Frederic Eden's A Garden in Venice *in 1903.*

unsympathetic new features are added.' Then he just about redeemed his subject: 'It requires all the good points of Shepherd's Gate to carry off these sacrifices to convenience. Luckily, in the general amenity of the place they pass almost unnoticed.'

The house was built at the upper end of a substantial plot, with most of the gardens sloping down to the west and north, enjoying captivating views of the forested hills. A fashionable pergola made of larch poles stretched out along the high ground to the south, terminating in a thatch-roofed hut by the garden boundary. (The path is just visible between the piers of a porte-cochère in the picture above.) It is strongly reminiscent of the pergola described by Frederic Eden, Gertrude Jekyll's brother-in-law, in his book *A Garden in Venice* (1903). Eden's pergola – of a type that was cheap and simple to erect and captivating when lined with Madonna lilies – inspired many English copies.

Just a thin wedge of lawn and shrubbery separated the pergola from the hedged boundary at the top of the garden; but away from the house the sloping ground was carefully divided and levelled into several spacious terraces, enclosed by hedges or dry stone retaining walls. Within the enclosures were lawns and flower borders, rose gardens, a large orchard and kitchen gardens.

Among the roses were some of the great favourites of the period: soft-pink 'Mme Caroline Testout', one of the early hybrid teas dating from 1890; the white but scentless hybrid perpetual 'Frau Karl Druschki'; and old tea roses such as deep-pink 'Papa Gontier' and the white-with-pink-edge 'Homère'. On the west side, an avenue of standard roses sprang out of a sea of carnations either side of a brick footpath leading to the house.

It was Mrs Hutchinson who took a great interest in the garden, which is not surprising, for she was the definition of a 'golf widow'. Her husband, a crack amateur player, had won the British amateur championship in 1886 (he was the first Englishman to do so) and again the following year. He was also the first Englishman to be captain of the Royal and Ancient, and naturally had chosen a home where there were fine golf courses virtually on the doorstep. Hutchinson was widely admired for the way he could write prolifically on the subject of golf 'with style and grace', but he was also a regular correspondent on a number of other sporting interests – cricket, shooting, fishing and big game hunting, as well as history and natural history. There must have been very little time left to notice the roses and lilies.

Mrs Hutchinson was praised for turning the none-too-fertile soil of her garden into land that yielded second crops, with all the produce being of the highest quality. The kitchen gardens were extensive, considering the size of the house, and edged with rows of magnificent sweet peas and other cutting-garden flowers; they were most likely the favourites of the period – dahlias and delphiniums, gladioli, pyrethrums and peonies. Interestingly, Mrs Hutchinson credited the high quality of the sweet peas to her use of 'Nitro-bacterine', which suggests she took an active interest in the latest scientific discoveries being applied to farm crops – in this case, the inoculation of seeds with symbiotic nitrogen-fixing bacteria.

Shepherd's Gate's garden, with its hierarchy of spaces, embraced many of Gertrude Jekyll's enthusiasms, including the poking of alpine plants into the crevices of dry stone walls. And it would have been representative of many readers' experiences, being a practical, family amenity with space to kick a ball (perhaps even to chip-and-putt one) and grow fresh produce and flowers. It is believed that Miss Jekyll had a hand in its creation – as regular contributors to *Country Life*, she and Hutchinson were colleagues – though the extent of her involvement is not clear. In spite of the many enchanting photographs of the garden taken in 1909 by *Country Life*, only a misty detail of yew trees was published in the Jekyll and Weaver book *Gardens for Small Country Houses*, published in 1912.

Today, a portion of the grounds has been sold off and many of the old features (including all of those shown here) have completely disappeared, though the bones of an Edwardian garden can still be seen in some paths and dry stone walls.

Cool shade in high summer under the pergola. Substantial flower gardens and lawns, enclosed by hedges, were laid out to the west and north.

MUNTHAM COURT, SUSSEX

A few miles north of the seaside town of Worthing, Muntham Court was a mysterious mansion, set in a scenic wooded landscape amid the ash trees and yews of the South Downs. Indeed, the preponderance of dark yews in its garden, shaped into arcaded hedges and towering cones, seemed to add to its layers of intrigue. Even in 1906 when these pictures were taken, there is a suggestion of melancholy in the air, though the property at that date was still lavishly tended and hosting entertainments and field sports on the grand scale. Iron Age settlements had been discovered in the vicinity of the house and also a Roman temple, which, when excavated in 1953–54, yielded many votive items and bones of sacrificial animals.

In 1743, a Georgian mansion of red brick was built at Muntham on the site of an earlier timber house for Anthony Browne, 6th Viscount Montagu. He was the owner of nearby Cowdray, but

Left: *The long Yew Walk seen from the Crown Garden, with its intricate pattern of box hedging, inspired by the embroidery design for a baby's cap.*

Below: *The vista from the Yew Walk, looking back to the house, focused on the large bay window of the drawing room at the north end of the east front.*

chiefly wanted Muntham as a hunting box. Around the house were laid out great plantations, rides and fishponds and, by 1754, water was brought 'with great expense' to the house. In this area of chalk downland, surface water is scarce and wells must plunge 200 feet or so into the rock to find it.

In 1765, the property, then encompassing 2,000 acres, was sold on to William Frankland, a descendant of Oliver Cromwell on his mother's side and the son of a governor of Fort William, Calcutta. Though he greatly extended the house, Frankland, an inventor and scientist, must have been too busy with all his other enthusiasms to take a great interest in the gardens, though he did enlarge the fishponds. Born in Bengal in 1720, he had become a wealthy East India Company merchant, and, before settling in Sussex, he spent three dangerous years travelling in disguise as a Turkish messenger, exploring Persia and the Ottoman Empire, Baghdad and the recently revealed ruins of Palmyra in the Syrian desert, and then Damascus and Jerusalem. Once safely settled in Muntham, he stayed until his death forty years later, meanwhile devoting his time and the rooms of the house to an extraordinary collection of machinery, including clocks and watches, lathes, printing machines, cloth looms and much else. His researches into newfangled

machines and mechanical inventions apparently cost him more than £20,000 – a princely sum; the entire Muntham Estate had cost him just £6,300.

In 1850, Muntham was sold to the Dowager Marchioness of Bath, who settled in Sussex once her eldest son was old enough to take over the estates at Longleat. It had potential, but apparently the widow of Bath muttered, 'The upper classes do not live in red brick.' She therefore employed architect Henry Woodyer to restyle the house in the Neo-Jacobean manner, extending it to the south, adding high gables to the roof-line and refacing all the elevations with the grey knapped flints so abundant in this region.

New gardens were created in the enclosed and absolutely up-to-date 'old-fashioned' style, with hedges grown high separating rectangular green courts. The most interesting and ambitious area was the Crown Garden, laid out for the Dowager Marchioness in front of a terrace beside the east elevation of the house. From its centrepiece statue, an intricate pattern radiated out in circles and swirls of dwarf box hedging, with gravelled paths weaving around beds of seasonal flowers and spiky-leaved agaves. The pattern is said to have been taken from an embroidery design for the crown of a baby's cap. The splendid view from a large bay window of the drawing room at the north end of the east front took in the Crown Garden, then a vista down the tall-hedged Yew Walk, terminating, if one could see it, in a semicircular enclosure several hundred yards away. Around the crown pattern, box and yew topiaries of varied shapes agreeably reinforced the suggestion of a seventeenth-century pleasance.

For a house of its size and gardens of such stature, there must have been considerable backup in the shape of glasshouses and kitchen gardens. Beyond the arcaded hedges of the east gardens and the main entrance drive on the north side, mature trees planted by earlier generations included conifers from the New World, plus cedars, Continental pines, and novelties such as monkey-puzzle and weeping beech.

When *Country Life* featured Muntham Court in February 1907, it was the home of Lady Ulrica Thynne, the widowed daughter-in-law of the Dowager Marchioness. After Lady Ulrica's death in 1916, her son, Colonel Ulric Oliver Thynne, was the last owner. As a sporting man with particular interests in hunting and racing, he did little to change the gardens, though for a while a pair of elegant wrought-iron gates from Seville Cathedral, believed to have been plundered in 1812 during the Peninsular War, were erected at the East Lodge entrance.

During the Second World War, the Army occupied the estate, and after Colonel Thynne's death in 1957, the house and its gardens became derelict. Early in 1961, the breakers moved in for Sussex County Council and Muntham Court and its gardens were flattened. It is now the site of Worthing Crematorium.

Magnificent arcaded hedges also lined the main drive up to the north front of the house, whose walls had been refaced with flints.

SEDGWICK PARK, SUSSEX

One of the most fascinating and original gardens created in the late years of Victoria's reign was at Sedgwick Park, some 300 feet above sea level in the undulating countryside of the Sussex Weald. Compared with some of its contemporaries, Sedgwick Park's garden also had a long innings, getting better and better as it matured for four decades under the guiding hand of its creator, Emma Henderson. *Country Life* has a particularly good photographic record of the property, as it was featured five times between 1901 and 1957, well before the garden went into decline.

In ancient times, the St Leonard's Forest area in which Sedgwick is situated was part of the Saxon rape of Bramber. Through turbulent times the locality underwent many different ownerships and tenancies; at one stage, in 1249, the manor at Sedgwick, as it now came to be called, was leased to John Maunsell, Treasurer of York, Prior of Beverley and 'Chancellor in all but name' to Henry III. 'This warrior-cleric, this *éminence grise*,' wrote Christopher Hussey in 1942, 'occupied a position behind the third Henry's throne comparable to Wolsey's behind the eighth's.' Remote Sedgwick, in the obscurity of forests thick with ancient oaks where few roads or tracks penetrated, acquired a fortified and crenellated castle, surrounded by two concentric moats – a useful retreat for a man with some powerful enemies.

Over succeeding centuries of power struggles Sedgwick manor – its castle and its hunting grounds – was broken up, passing through the hands of several families including that of the Duke of Norfolk. It was Robert and Emma Henderson who transformed Sedgwick Park into the fine home it became in the late nineteenth century. Robert Henderson, a director of the Bank of England, inherited the estate in 1871 from his father, and employed the fashionable London architectural practice of Ernest George and Harold Peto to design a new house, which was built in 1886.

Creation of the garden must have followed soon after. *Country Life*'s photographs of *c*.1900 showed the yew hedges already well grown – luxuriant from top to bottom, crisply edged and standing a good deal taller than the lady (presumably Emma Henderson) positioned enigmatically beside them (see page 9). With good cultivation it would take yews a minimum of twelve years to achieve such stature, which suggests a planting date of *c*.1887.

Mrs Henderson has usually been credited as the sole creator of the garden. Yet Sedgwick's bare bones suggest an architect's – particularly Peto's – rigorous influence. A generously spacious terrace on the south front creates a dominant central vista leading to formal pools, which reflect the sky, and drawing the eye to the distant horizon of the South Downs. Hilly ground to the east is levelled out into well-proportioned compartments of lawned terraces and arrow-straight walks. They are linked by stone stairways; vistas are terminated with inviting seats moulded into wall niches. The sequence has a satisfying unity, easing the visitor into the site without any overbearing self-consciousness. Sedgwick's layout hints at ideas which are consummately put into practice in Peto's subsequent designs at Buscot Park, at his own Iford Manor and at Bridge House, Weybridge.

'Quaint and curious is the idea of likening the house and garden to a ship of the Royal Navy,' remarked the author of the 1901 *Country Life* feature, and this is one of the remarkable oddities of Sedgwick: the garden was divided up like a great ship, with its different areas nautically labelled. 'The Upper Deck' was a long walk at the top, east side of the garden; 'The Quarter Deck' was a parallel walk along the terrace below it; 'The Bulwarks' were a series of topiarised buttresses laid against a wall between Quarter and Upper Decks. 'The Portholes' were elliptical holes cut through a tall yew hedge separating two more levelled areas (which became rose gardens during Lord Rotherwick's ownership in the 1950s). The formal, rectangular pool in the south slope became 'The White Sea', being a bright mirror of the wide open skies; a loggia set into the wall at one end of the pool was labelled 'The Chief Cabin'. The house, with its sweeping views down the garden from upstairs, was of course 'The Masthead'.

When *Country Life* returned to Sedgwick in 1927, it noted the ideal aspect, with the gardens taking full advantage of their sunny, south-facing slope. On the west side, it recorded the 'elm walk with a magnificent herbaceous border in front backed by arches smothered with ramblers; still farther lies the iris walk, long with narrow borders and a background of clipped hedges'. Mrs Henderson planted clear-stemmed holm oaks, *Quercus ilex*, on

Above: *In this view looking back to the house, taken in 1942, the White Sea is covered with water lilies and marginal plants.*

Right: *Stretching out southwards from the house, the formal gardens as they were in 1942, framed by great pines, with the South Downs in the distance.*

Following pages: *In maturity, the rock banks and water garden took on a Japanese character, softening the impact of the crisp hedges.*

the slope below the terraces east of the house, 'with beds filled with roses and the normal summer bedding plants nestling below them ... . The result is exactly the same as that given by a garden in an olive grove on the Riviera.' It had been seen nowhere else in an English garden, declared the author.

As the garden matured, the White Sea took on a Japanese theme, with lantern ornaments and a crane. It became a luxuriant home for water lilies, its straight edges obscured by ferns, phormiums, *Iris sibirica*, candelabra and *sikkimensis* primulas, rodgersias and *Cotoneaster horizontalis*. Cracks between the huge slabs of home-quarried 'crazy' paving on the house terrace nurtured clouds of *Campanula carpatica* and a lollipop of honeysuckle. Steep banks either side of the White Sea were fashioned into rock gardens planted 'in enormous variation', and also with Mrs Henderson's signature white-flowered yuccas, which were distributed all over Sedgwick's gardens in bold groups.

What became of Sedgwick Park? In the late decades of the twentieth century, the estate plunged into a low period, exchanging hands several times and being plundered along the way for any-thing that was feasibly removable. Unscrupulous owners removed seats, statues, urns and ornaments from the gardens; light fittings, fireplaces and pretty door ironmongery disappeared from the house. The grounds, once so lovingly manicured – in Mrs Henderson's day there were eight gardeners – became seriously neglected and overgrown. Parcels of land were sold off. Nearly all the flower gardens disappeared and the lavish dark-green and golden yews lost all identifiable shape where they were not actually cut down. Now, things look more hopeful. Sedgwick is in new and sympathetic ownership and the intention is to refurbish or restore much of the house and grounds in the coming years.

Above: *A huge* Quercus ilex *tree and Mrs Henderson's signature yuccas rise out of the crazy-paving terrace, framing the view down the Quarter Deck walk.*

Right: *The Upper Deck was a long walk on high ground east of the house, passing under alternating arches of yew and vines.*

VALEWOOD FARM, SUSSEX

Like Compton End (pages 42–7), Valewood Farm was featured in *Country Life*'s long-running series of 'Lesser Country Houses of To-day', which included coverage of the ever-increasing trend for weekend cottages. Affordable second homes were, of course, a rich seam for *Country Life* to tap into editorially, having the beneficial side effect of increasing regular readership among the middle classes, while generating masses of extra advertising revenue.

So the pretty, tile-hung cottage of Valewood Farm, which had been painted several times by Helen Allingham at the turn of the century with a climbing rose garlanding the doorway and white doves settled on its roof, was studied for two comprehensive articles – on 13 October 1928 and 21 September 1935. In both features, the doves still fluttered around the great chimney-stack, though by 1935 they were being upstaged by magnificent peacocks. Comparison of an Allingham watercolour – featuring a peasant

Above: The farmhouse was a veritable menagerie, retaining much of the character that had inspired Helen Allingham's watercolours.

Left: Oliver Hill's genius was to turn the farmyard buildings into stylish open-air loggias, while keeping to cottage-garden vernacular in the paths.

girl at the gate framed by simple sunflowers and bunched-up marguerites – with the sophisticated *Country Life* articles of three decades later neatly demonstrates the post-First World War gentrification of humble farmsteads into stylish country homes.

Also, like Compton End, Valewood Farm was owned by an architect, in this case Oliver Hill, whose work was occasionally featured in the magazine. Mr Hill had long searched for a suitable property before acquiring the cottage with its 300-year-old solid walls of local sandstone and a much more ancient, timber interior. As part of the domain of Valewood House, Mr Hill's land occupied a long rectangular section between old brick walls, with one wall lining the lane and its opposite parallel a retaining wall set against the west-facing hillside, with clouds of dark hollies ranged above the copings. A huge old ash tree beside the house loomed and groaned over its roof just like the great wych elm of E. M. Forster's *Howards End*.

The farmyard, with its crowd of barn, byre, dovecote and granary, created a spacious rectangular courtyard into which the architect installed an oval swimming pool, axially lined up with the house entrance at one end and a path to a seat at the other, with the cross axis leading to airy loggias. It was a masterpiece of simple and coherent design which maintained the dignity of the vernacular buildings, while giving them a fresh use as places for al fresco dining or breezy, informal shelter from the sun.

Swimming pools were still a comparatively rare luxury in England at this time, and Oliver Hill's elliptical design, 5 feet 6 inches deep, 30 feet long and 20 feet wide with whitened, sloping sides, was daringly modern but beautifully executed. It was conveniently fed by a natural spring and its water was an amazing azure blue, due to occasional applications of copper sulphate. 'Whether this is a desirable chemical to swallow when swimming in the pool is a moot point for the chemist to decide, but Mr Hill seems to thrive on his constant plunges into it,' remarked Randal Phillips, the author of the 1928 article. This azure theme was carried through the garden with blue-glazed Spanish pots of varied shapes, placed carefully around the pool, at doorways and within the loggias. The pool was designed to be always brim-full, with any overspill of water gently and efficiently carried away into the ever-so-slightly cambered brick edging, which concealed a drain.

Planting was in the sophisticated-country-cottage style that had already been prescribed for three decades by Gertrude Jekyll. In fact, Miss Jekyll herself was engaged by Mr Hill to provide planting plans for Valewood Farm. It was a late commission for her, just prior to *Country Life*'s 1928 visit. Although many of her suggestions were initially carried out, in Christopher Hussey's 1935 feature he noted that 'the garden, which Mr Hill has designed and largely planted himself, is interesting for the pictorial use made of ordinary plants and common materials. ... [it] is a small but notable example of the "impressionistic" style associated with Miss Jekyll, who, indeed, supplied the original planting plan for the main beds. This has been largely departed from in the course of time ...'. Jekyll plants there were, though, in masses of delphiniums, anchusas and *Salvia virgata* – again picking up the blue theme – 'relieved by pink sidalcea and grey foliage plants'.

The vista from the house led the eye past a sentinel pair of cypress trees (which predated Oliver Hill's arrival), through the swimming pool, thence through the barn, whose doors had been removed, opening up the view down a path through meadow grass, and ending in a ha-ha with parkland views beyond. 'The planting on either side of the walk is predominantly of evergreens and "evergreys",' observed Hussey. These last were in silvery drifts of santolina, senecio and *Stachys byzantina*, interrupted by 'somewhat overhanging' prostrate junipers. 'This permanent furnishing is interspersed with masses of lupins to the right, backed by a dense screen of brooms, lilacs, gorse, and beech, with the tall umbrellas of giant cow parsley ...'. The potential for great variety in the flowers was compromised by the presence of the peacocks – so wallflowers, pinks, stocks, aubrietas and annual flowers that habitually were the blooms of the country cottage had to be sacrificed.

Blue, silver and white featured strongly in the planting, with much use of Gertrude Jekyll's favourite delphiniums, campanulas, eryngiums and stachys.

Apart from the bucolic charm of the cottage and Hill's delightful menagerie therein, the garden at Valewood is interesting because it serves as a visual and emotional catalyst, linking the Edwardian sensibilities of Lutyens and Jekyll with the new, dynamic Modernism of the post-First World War period. Coming from a wealthy and well-connected family, Hill was a generation younger than Edwin Lutyens, but the latter, a family friend who lived nearby when Hill was growing up, was for many years his mentor.

Lutyens had advised Hill to take his first job upon leaving school not at any academy, but in a builder's yard, where he would learn about construction materials through hands-on experience. After eighteen months he was ready to be articled in the architectural office of William Flockhart (1854–1913), where he would spend three years, and from 1909 to 1911 he attended the Architectural Association's evening school for tuition in drawing.

A big break came for Hill in 1910–13 with a commission for remodelling the house and creating elaborate gardens at Moor Close, Binfield, in Berkshire, for C. Birch Crisp Esq., a wealthy

Left and below: *Swimming pools were still a rare luxury in 1920s gardens. Hill's elliptical pool was dyed azure blue with doses of copper sulphate.*

businessman. The Moor Close scheme, with its rills, gazebos, statues, steps, balustrades, ponds, pergolas and varied pavings, displayed the excesses of an inexperienced designer who has not yet learned that less can be more and who feels the need to put all his inspirational eggs into one groaning basket.

But by the time Hill arrived at Valewood in the mid-1920s, the Great War had intervened, his work had matured and he was able to jettison some of the excessive cosiness of his Edwardian apprenticeship in favour of a braver, modern worldview, illustrated by the clear blue elliptic pool set in an open and uncluttered lawn. As Hill's own style developed, the influence of Lutyens was usurped by the pure Modernism of the Finnish architect Alvar Aalto; in parallel with this, *Country Life*'s enthusiasm for Modernist design also increased during the 1930s, providing a showcase for the sleek white villas and plate-glass windows of Hill's homes for wealthy clients.

After the Second World War, Hill moved to the Cotswolds, and Valewood was turned back into a working farm; the gardens and vernacular buildings completely disappeared. The present owners are painstakingly restoring the cottage, but sadly the garden is entirely lost.

SWAYLANDS, KENT

Swaylands, just south of Penshurst in Kent, was among the most ambitious gardens of its kind, captured in its maturity when *Country Life* visited in 1906. In a setting of little hills clouded with oak and beech woods, the house was set upon a hilltop, with the grounds gently sloping into a valley. Levelled terraces were laid out near the house: the top terrace being devoted to a lime-tree walk, second and third terraces nurturing borders of 'old-world' flowers and the fourth providing access to the owner's private cricket ground, edged with craggy oak trees. Beyond that, and the pretty apple orchard, lay the exciting chasms of the rock garden. While one path took a circuit that swept around a lake, other routes wove their way up and down through the man-made geological wonder.

It was the creation of the owner, Mr George Drummond, and his gardener, Hosier. It was a remarkable feat to pile up the natural

Above: The sandstone rock garden at Swaylands was among the most ambitious to be attempted anywhere, with alpine flowers planted in luxuriant profusion.

Left: Seas of daffodils ornamented the apple orchard in early spring, followed by wild flowers self-sown in the meadow grass.

sandstones, 'many of them nine tons in weight', into hundreds of yards of walks. Their fissures were artlessly planted with tumbling flowers such as North American alpine phlox – 'not in driblets but in large groups' and in great variety, arabis, pinky-white *Gypsophila repens*, mustard-yellow *Alyssum saxatile* and vivid mauve aubrietas. There were also rare treasures, such as the streptocarpus-like *Haberlea rhodopensis*, the not-really-alpine white bells of *Ostrowskia magnifica*, and a colony of the native lady's-slipper orchid, *Cypripedium calceolus*, which even then was noted as being 'now almost extinct'. Trees and shrubs were the latest from Veitch's Nursery, and some conifers, doubtless planted as 'dwarfs', were already getting way out of scale for the setting.

In 1919, George Drummond sold Swaylands to a hospital, and the stables were converted into nurses' homes in 1927. During the Second World War, the building was used as a military hospital, after which it became a special school. After lying empty since 1994, Swaylands is currently being converted and carved up into a development of private apartments and houses, though there are plans to restore the rock garden, which has for so long been lost among trees and brambles.

ESHER PLACE, SURREY

Esher Place survives today in name only, as an upmarket housing estate, but a century ago it was the seat of Sir Edgar Vincent, a glamorous Orientalist whose linguistic expertise had led him into a colourful overseas career of diplomacy and finance, including sorting out the economy of Egypt and negotiating with Armenian terrorists who had taken hostages at the Ottoman Bank. With its neighbourhood of elegant country houses, horse-racing at Sandown Park on the doorstep, and easy access to the City of London, it is easy to see why, in 1895, the Vincents decided upon Esher Place.

The first house dated back to the eleventh century but was replaced by William Wayneflete, Bishop of Winchester, in the fifteenth century. Cardinal Wolsey enlarged it in 1528 and added a fine gatehouse by the river. A drawing of c.1700 by Johannes Kip shows Esher Place having vast formal gardens, hedged and enclosed, with straight avenues and a huge canal. William Kent relandscaped the grounds for Henry Pelham, Prime Minister to George II, but in 1805 the next owner demolished all but Wolsey's gatehouse and built a new home on higher ground.

Besides rebuilding the house, the Vincents made extensive new gardens incorporating walled kitchen and fruit grounds, herbaceous borders and cut-flower beds, a rose garden and a lavender walk. The flowers included tiger lilies, hollyhocks, lupins, poppies, heliotropes and sweet peas. In 1905, Edwin Lutyens was commissioned to design a small water garden with formal pools and a rill.

When the Vincents left Esher in 1930, the estate became a development site, though the Lutyens garden was attached to one new house and Wolsey's gatehouse survives as a separate home. The main house is a headquarters and training centre for one of the trade unions.

Above: *Viewed across the park, beyond Lady Vincent's flower gardens, Cardinal Wolsey's gatehouse stands alone in the landscape beside the River Mole.*

Left: *Magnificent trees and elegant turf steps enclosed the croquet lawn of Sir Edgar Vincent's political power base at Esher.*

THREE

THAMES & CHILTERNS

A century ago, competitive horticulture, financed by family banks, reached its zenith on the alkaline soils north of the Thames. At the Rothschilds' Gunnersbury Park estate (*below*), no expense was spared in order to help the head gardener, James Hudson, raise the best produce for the show bench, and there were no rivals. None, that is, other than those grown by Edwin Beckett, head gardener at Aldenham House, belonging to the Gibbs family of merchant bankers. Those two great gardens were among the most famous of their day. Very different and ultimately more influential was Norah Lindsay's celebrated (and uncompetitive) garden on Oxfordshire limestone at Sutton Courtenay Manor; its *laissez-faire* style informed gardening taste throughout the twentieth century. Somewhere between the two poles sits Wittington (*left*), the passion of Lord Devonport. With its steep, flinty paths, lavish rock garden and luxuriant herbaceous borders, it was one of the most admired gardens of the 1920s.

WITTINGTON, BUCKINGHAMSHIRE

Occupying a spectacular hillside site above the River Thames near Henley, Wittington was the archetypal nineteenth-century plutocrat's residence, being within comfortable reach of London but set within an enviably scenic landscape. It was the home of Hudson Ewbanke Kearley, a tea merchant and grocer, who founded the lucrative chain of International Stores and became Viscount Devonport before the close of the First World War.

Lord Devonport was passionate and knowledgeable about his garden. It was laid out in grassy terraces around the house, with serene lawns and two rows of clipped yews separating a pair of magnificent herbaceous borders panning out from the west front. An open valley sheltered by shrubberies and handsome trees ran down the hill towards the river. The garden's steep gradient was handled exceptionally well; several elegant stairways with comfortably easy risers were created to provide access up and down. A notable feature of two of these was the decorative manner in which flat pieces of flint were pressed into concrete along the edge of each step, while the inner part of the step was turfed. This gave the steps a practical but natural appearance within the broader landscape and also complemented the local geology.

The most spectacular area was a huge rock garden below a chalky cliff, laced with little paths like goat tracks through a stony Cretan hillside. Planting was in bold swathes, with choice species such as *Anemone baldensis* and *Shortia galacifolia* forming thick colonies several feet wide, tucked into peaty soil between the rocks. The Pyrenean crevice-dweller *Ramonda myconi* was observed in 1927 to grow 'like a weed'; *Tropaeolum polyphyllum* trailed swags of yellow flowers over the boulders. At the very bottom, a wild bog and water garden was skilfully planted in a water meadow, with willows and bamboo plus flag and *sibirica* irises.

Wittington today is a reduced estate of 80 acres, owned by a software company. Much work has recently been carried out in regenerating the flower gardens around the house. The outer areas, including the rock garden and stairways, are presently lost under woodland trees and ivy, though there is the intention to uncover them eventually.

Above: *The River Thames, glimpsed through some of the fine trees at Wittington. Lord Devonport's cherished rock garden is in the foreground.*

Right: *Owing to the steep gradient, several elegant stairways were fashioned, giving access to a bog garden skilfully planted in the water meadows below.*

GUNNERSBURY PARK, MIDDLESEX

Gunnersbury was the first major Rothschild garden created in England and it also became one of the most famous, such was the care and expenditure lavished upon it.

Its name is believed to derive from King Canute's niece, Gunhilda, and the estate was occupied in turn by Alice Perrers, a mistress of Edward III, and later George II's daughter, Princess Amelia. A Palladian house built in the seventeenth century was demolished in 1801, whereupon the estate was divided into thirteen redevelopment plots. Lot 1, a rectangular strip running north-west to south-east, on the north-eastern corner of the old estate, was bought by one Stephen Cosser; the other twelve lots were bought by Alexander Copeland, a builder. Gunnersbury House, a pretty villa, was built on Lot 1, on a gentle eminence sloping down to the

Above: Gunnersbury House, the second (and smaller) mansion. The two houses were built side by side, on top of a gentle, south-facing slope.

Left: Suggesting the elegance of an Italian palazzo, the western entrance to the terrace in front of Gunnersbury Park, the larger of the two mansions.

south. Right next door to it, on Lot 2, the slightly larger Gunnersbury Park was erected by Copeland, but he never went on to build houses on the remaining plots. Instead, following his death in 1834, Gunnersbury Park was sold in 1835 along with the remaining former building plots (totalling 80 acres) to Nathan Rothschild.

Though they had to put up with having a neighbour's villa right on their doorstep, the Rothschilds set about improving their house and park with the help of architect Sydney Smirke. A fine stable block was added, and an elegant orangery with a high glass roof. The latter became the home of huge tree ferns more than 33 feet tall – a gift from the Governor of Tasmania in 1873.

Gunnersbury's gently sloping park of lawns and trees, with its circular pool at the north end overlooked by a Classical temple (both thought to be by William Kent; see frontispiece), offered distinct possibilities. Princess Amelia had spent a small fortune on the grounds, but most of her garden buildings had been demolished for the 1801 sale. More large trees were planted in the 1840s by Baron Lionel de Rothschild to augment existing handsome cedars and elms; roses were splendidly displayed, with a series of basket-

style beds set into the lawns. Other rose beds created blocks of colour: a single bed of clear pink 'Caroline Testout' roses contained as many as 600 bushes.

The Rothschilds bought land adjoining Gunnersbury in the 1840s and 1860s, increasing the estate to well over 600 acres. And in 1889, Leopold de Rothschild was at last able to buy Gunnersbury House (Lot 1) and patch up the hole in the old estate.

Gunnersbury was well watered. An ancient horseshoe lake became famous for its water lilies – more than fifty different varieties were fanned out over the water, flecking the lake with brilliant stars in white, deep red, shades of rose-pink and pale yellow. The acquired land to the south included a clay pit, which was flooded to form 'The Potomac' – a lake with an island.

When *Country Life* visited Gunnersbury in the autumn of 1900, it found the late-season flower borders every bit as impressive in autumn as they would have been through the summer, being richly furnished with red and golden dahlias, rudbeckias, Michaelmas daisies, chrysanthemums, strong yellow sunflowers and 'the best of all tiger lilies' – the reddish-orange turk's-cap *Lilium tigrinum* (var. *splendens*). Stone urns were filled with hybrid tea roses and special attention was paid to 'tub gardening' – the elaborate filling-out of large planters with seasonal flowers that were set at evenly spaced intervals along the terraces. Fragrant tubs were filled to bursting point with lemon verbenas, myrtles and scarlet Cape pelargoniums. Bay trees, orange trees, pomegranates, fuchsias, silver-leaved euonymus and veronicas were also given the tub treatment; the elegant containers, designed by Leopold de Rothschild himself, were square in shape, made from pitch pine and carefully lined with slate so that the roots had no contact with the timber.

Gunnersbury was also famous for its fruit. Pineapples were grown in variety, the most fabulous of which were named Providence, whose individual fruits could weigh up to 15 pounds. The head gardener in the early twentieth century was James Hudson, who held the Royal Horticultural Society's highest decoration – the Victoria Medal of Honour. Under Hudson's direction, 1,200 fruit trees were grown in rotating pots under glass to produce the maximum variety and the longest possible fruiting season, and his list of subjects grown is instructive: 'Of peaches: Alexander and Hale's Early, for early forcing; Early Grosse Mignonne, Dr Hogg, Sea Eagle and the Nectarine Peach. Nectarines: Cardinal, Early Rivers', Lord Napier. Pineapple: Victoria and Albert Victor. Plums: Early Prolific, Jefferson, Early Transparent, Golden Transparent, Coe's Golden Drop and Reine Claude de Bavay. Cherries: Guigne d'Annonay, Bigarreau de Schreken, Early Rivers', Frogmore Early Bigarreau, Governor Wood and Belle d'Orléans, with a tree of May Duke variety for the purposes of pollen. Pears: Fondante d'Automne, Conference, Doyenné du Comice, Pitmaston Duchess, Marie Louise and

Summer on the terrace at Gunnersbury Park. Lawns sloping down to the left led to the horseshoe lake, with its fine orangery at the waterside.

Durondeau. Apples: Ribston Pippin, Cox's Orange Pippin, Washington, King of Tompkins' County, Mabbott's Pearmain and Allington Pippin.' A disciplined system was maintained, so that after early forced peaches and nectarines had cropped, melons followed, and then pot figs; after pot cherries, plums (not forced) and other fruits followed, with pot-grown strawberries kept upon the greenhouse shelves.

Near the greenhouses, a special rectangular tank was devoted to cultivating bright-blue *Nymphaea stellata*, the tender water lilies of South East Asia, for cutting and displaying indoors. The tank was heated by a return pipe from the glasshouse boiler so that plentiful starry blooms were grown from early summer until the autumn.

In 1900, *Country Life* particularly admired Gunnersbury's waterside bamboo garden. The following year, James Hudson extended its oriental atmosphere into a full-scale Japanese garden, complete with a bamboo tea-house, a parade of lanterns and other suitable ornaments. It rapidly became one of the most celebrated 'Japanese' gardens in the country, with a bridge trailing white wisteria and stepping-stone paths winding between cherry blossoms

and the foliage of acers and aralia. Apparently, this was the garden that, when it was shown to a visiting Imperial ambassador, prompted the famous exclamation: 'Marvellous! We have nothing like it in Japan.'

When it was the turn of the next generation, Lionel de Rothschild, Leopold's son, bought land on the shores of the Solent and made his mark by creating the famous rhododendron gardens of Exbury, Hampshire. Leopold died in 1917 while the Great War was still raging, and Gunnersbury's estate was subsequently broken up and sold. It was truly the end of an era.

In 1925, the local authorities bought 190 acres of the estate to create an urban public park, which survives. Many key garden features have gone, though the two mansions now house an arts centre and a museum among serene lawns and beautiful trees.

Above: *The horseshoe lake, with one of the houses visible through the trees. The Rothschilds planted large trees to give the park a sense of maturity.*

Right: *A special heated tank was built to cultivate tender blue water lilies,* Nymphaea stellata, *which ornamented the houses from spring to autumn.*

ALDENHAM HOUSE, HERTFORDSHIRE

In the space of sixty years, the gardens of Aldenham House evolved to become one of the great horticultural spectacles of the late nineteenth and early twentieth centuries, tended by a hundred gardeners. This was due to the uncompromising devotion of three men: Henry Hucks Gibbs (the first Lord Aldenham), his youngest son, Vicary Gibbs, and their inimitable head gardener, Edwin Beckett, who arrived in 1884 and stayed for fifty years.

Henry Hucks Gibbs, who was Governor of the Bank of England from 1875 to 1877, came to Aldenham in 1869, inheriting a mid-seventeenth-century brick house set in mainly flat Hertfordshire parkland on unpromising soils of chalk and cold, stiff clay. In laying out the grounds in a way appropriate to a gentleman of his standing, he was inspired by a great avenue of elm trees which marched imposingly for several hundred yards straight up to the door on the west front. The elms, by then at least two hundred years old, were a magnificent feature in the landscape, fully mature and planted in a quincunx formation – that is, each row was arranged in multiple groups of five, like the five dots on a dice.

Henry Gibbs set out to acquire extra parcels of land to make the estate more cohesive, and from 1872 he created new serpentine access routes through the south-east and north-east sides of the park to reach the Elstree Road (which at that point is also the Roman road of Watling Street). There were still more adjustments to be made regarding access, however. To the north, Gibbs diverted the High Road, taking the old one and its trees into his park and creating a new public road further north. The new road, while being set a more seemly distance from the house, was also excavated 10 feet deep into the ground to ensure the Aldenham views were uninterrupted by 'traffic'. In the process, Gibbs also made the unpopular decision to demolish the Wrestlers, the local public house, though he built another on the new road junction and called it 'The Battleaxes', a name inspired not by any Gibbs matriarchs but by the family coat of arms.

The Gibbses, father and son, planted on a huge scale, creating extensive woods and avenues with straight vistas carving through the shrubberies and extending into the vast estates beyond the 200-acre park. Nevertheless, it was not all straight lines and symmetry; there was plenty of water available and the clay soil was easily puddled into impervious pool liners. So a boating lake with two islands was created south-east of the house, with one of the carriage driveways coasting over it via a substantial bridge. The acquired land to the north incorporated ancient moats and a stew pond, which presented the opportunity of creating scenic and more intimate water gardens. The firm of James Pulham, famous for their Pulhamite (a sort of reconstituted stone) rock formations, was employed for some years at Aldenham, laying out bridges, stony weirs across the stream, and other rock and water landscapes.

Absolute perfection was maintained in the 15-acre pleasure gardens by a vast army of gardeners. It was said that of all the rare plants, the rarest was a weed.

Yet these are just the outer areas; the 15 acres of main pleasure gardens were set within an area enclosed by the ha-ha, topped by a low wall. A formal garden of perfectly symmetrical flowerbeds surrounded by gravel walks lay near the east front of the house. Beyond it, down a short flight of steps, there was a magnificent rose garden enclosed by topiarised yew hedges, with a lead sundial centrepiece.

The contribution of Vicary Gibbs and Edwin Beckett to horticulture can hardly be overstated (and both of them were to receive the Victoria Medal of Honour from the Royal Horticultural Society). Beckett used the 2-acre walled kitchen garden to its maximum potential, especially for growing prize exhibition fruits and vegetables, though apparently this resulted in miserly portions of produce being sent up to the house for actual consumption. The prodigious quantities of fruit produced almost rivalled the Rothschilds at Gunnersbury.

Numerous new cultivars, both decorative and edible, were raised at Aldenham, with Gibbs winning more than a hundred gold medals from the RHS. On top of all its other wonders, Gibbs confidently declared Aldenham to have the best collection of hardy woody plants to be found in any private collection in the world. Certainly, there was no shortage of rare plants at Aldenham, though the *Kew Bulletin*'s obituary for Vicary Gibbs in 1932 observed that 'after a tour of the garden one always felt that a weed was probably the rarest'.

Edwin Beckett retired in 1932 and died in 1935. From 1934 the property was let, and the garden's contents were sold off in 1935. The BBC occupied Aldenham during the Second World War, and subsequently the house and part of the grounds were sold to a school. Only small traces of this once great garden remain, though there are many fine trees surrounding the playing fields.

Above: *The bathing pool, formerly a stew pond, with its rockwork changing locker and diving platform.*

Left: *The introduction of water gardens enlivened the level grounds. The prestigious firm of James Pulham & Son created many of the water and rock features.*

Sutton Courtenay Manor, Berkshire

Surely the greatest period for the grounds around the manor house at Sutton Courtenay was during the lifetime of Norah Lindsay (1866–1948), a naturally gifted gardener, glittering hostess, and friend of society *grandes dames* including Nancy Astor, Sibyl Colefax and Emerald Cunard.

Raised in Ireland, Norah came to Sutton Courtenay towards the close of the nineteenth century as the bride of Captain (later Colonel) Harry Lindsay. That the intelligent and sought-after Mrs Lindsay found time to tend her garden between an endless round of house parties and social gatherings is in itself remarkable; but maybe those demands elsewhere partly account for its influential laidback style, the other vital ingredient being her intuitive approach to the unspoilt surroundings. She wrote in *Country Life* in 1931, 'Every garden should be a continuation of the house it surrounds, and where the dwelling is old and sleepy the garden,

Above: The Lindsays preserved the 'cool green savannahs' of water meadows, the banks of which were fringed with kingcups and leucojums in the spring.

Left: Norah Lindsay beside the sundial in the circular entrance court. Her relaxed style of planting strongly influenced twentieth-century gardening.

too, must be drowsy and lie under the spell of the ages, so that you are conscious of the years that have given the grey stone walls their gold and the heavy yews their girth.'

Certainly, the manor house lay in a languorous spot, beside a lazy bend in a river feeding into the Thames south of Oxford. Surrounded by lush meadows naturally speckled with snake's-head fritillaries and kingcups, where the water's edge was fringed with osiers and the giant snowdrop flowers of leucojums, the location led Norah Lindsay to reflect that nature's work had always been more perfect than anything that she had done in the garden. 'Carefully have I preserved these cool green savannahs flowing serenely along the river's bank. Their solitude is refreshing after the crowded coloured gardens, and serves to allay the nostalgia at the heart of all humans for the lost wild places of their dreams. One step through the big watchful yews, down the long rose gallery, and you are in a sanctuary shared by the water-vole and the willow wren, inviolate as the meadows of Avalon.' Harry Lindsay, keen on ornithology, created a safe haven of islands and pools near the old mill, intended not for collecting but for preserving and increasing bird life.

So, in this privileged setting, Mrs Lindsay's home – hung with seventeenth-century tapestries and brocades and furnished with carved oak – radiated all the ancient character that a romantic soul could wish for. The house was a collection of medieval buildings arranged in a back-to-front 'C' shape around a flagstoned court-yard, with a high wall completing the fourth side on the west. Its east elevation faced out on to an oval entrance court with huge gate piers, beyond which a driveway lined with columnar yews cut through wild gardens up to the road. The west side had climbing roses over an unusual path punctuated with small tanks of minia-ture water lilies, leading down to the river less than 200 yards away. The Lindsays created gardens and walks and planted trees all over their estate, though Norah's celebrated flower gardens and topiaries rolled out from the south elevation of the house.

Occupying this south side were the rectangular Long Garden and a parallel Persian Garden, the two separated by a high stone wall. In the Long Garden, tall, free-growing yew trees near the house created a dark frame through which could be seen box-edged hoggin paths and beds dotted with clipped and bound Irish yews. Other yews were fashioned into the tiered 'cakestand' topiaries familiar from medieval woodcut illustrations. Gertrude Jekyll, a generation older than Norah, admired topiary but disapproved of clipping and training fastigiate yews, as she made plain when writing about St Catherine's Court; yet for Mrs Lindsay, they inspired thoughts of the tall, thin cypresses of Italian gardens she had admired in the countryside around Florence and Rome. At Sutton Courtenay she planted around them with a cottage gardener's abandon, using lupins, anchusas, mulleins, mallows, thalictrums, hollyhocks, tall campanulas and eremurus in big, comfortable drifts that were subtly embroidered by unexpected self-sown flowers.

The effect was of artless abundance but there was an underlying colour scheme that had been most carefully considered. So, rich blue flowers, deep purples and various pink and lemon tints were grown well apart from dazzling scarlet poppies, 'burning alstro-emerias', and the sharp, deep golds of rudbeckias and sunflowers. These last, hot-coloured flowers were instead winningly offset against the cooling effects of grey-leaved grasses, incense-and-grapefruit-scented *Salvia sclarea* (var. *turkestanica*), and the giant silvery thistle *Onopordum giganteum*.

It is a freer interpretation of herbaceous planting than the pillowy borders prescribed by Miss Jekyll, and photographs taken in about 1930 suggest that Norah Lindsay's flowers frequently breached the corsets of knee-high box hedging, since the latter appear riddled with gaps and holes. Within countless wall crevices, self-sown verbascums, anchusas and, above all, red and pink valerian were 'uninvited, though not unwelcome ... I have no heart to pull them up'.

The wall separating the Long Garden from the Persian Garden was garlanded with flowering shrubs and climbers: *Magnolia*

Lit by late-afternoon sunshine, the Long Garden's herbaceous flowers are punctuated by clipped Irish yews, reminiscent of Italian cypress trees.

grandiflora, Akebia quinata, golden pea-flowered *Piptanthus nepalensis,* white-flowered *Abutilon vitifolium,* hydrangea-like *Fendlera rupicola,* powder-blue ceanothus and many different clematis ensured colour and interest through the year.

The Persian Garden was reached via an old iron gate in the wall, engulfed by a sun-warmed tangle of pomegranate. Above all it was a fragrant rose garden with a hedge of the striped York and Lancaster rose near the house and a 10-foot-high screen of honeysuckle. Roses were planted in great profusion down the long beds, in mixed groups themed by colour so that reds, pinks and burgundies were kept separate from tangerine, lemon and cream flowered hybrids. The edges were thickly planted with clove-scented pinks. The garden ended in a timber alcove of grapevines whose fruits were turned by the devoted housekeeper into 'local vintage much enjoyed by the female members of the house'.

Norah Lindsay's informal garden style found favour among the fashionable set in which she circulated. Among them, Nancy Astor invited her to 'dress' Cliveden for the Ascot house parties; Norah also created planting schemes for Philip Sassoon at Port Lympne

and for the Trittons at Godmersham. She designed new gardens at Blickling Hall in Norfolk, where she was a frequent guest, and heavily influenced a carefree planting style at Hidcote, having become a close friend of Major Lawrence Johnston.

Of the Lindsays' two children, their daughter Nancy became an even greater plantswoman than Norah and lived out her life in the nearby Manor House Cottage. But that did not save the garden. The outgoings were huge and in 1945 Norah had to sell up. Sutton Courtenay was bought by her friend David Astor. Realising that Norah's garden could not survive without her, Astor soon employed Brenda Colvin, a rising star in landscape design, to rationalise the grounds. In the radical modernisation that ensued, Norah's gardens, including the dramatic oval entrance court, disappeared. The manor house remains in simplified but still tranquil grounds.

Right: *Valerian colonised the walls, as here at the top of the Persian Garden, with striped York and Lancaster roses close to the house.*

Below: *An elegant urn and medieval-looking topiaries in the Long Garden. Self-sown red valerian was left* in situ *if it created the right effect.*

KING'S HEAD HOUSE, BUCKINGHAMSHIRE

Country Life did not often feature town houses, other than the most elegant city homes, and very seldom town gardens. But King's Head House was an exception. As the name suggests, it was at one time a coaching inn, serving the old and wide main road of Beaconsfield in Buckinghamshire. Although it was originally a sixteenth-century oak-framed building (known in ancient times as Essex House), it underwent modifications in 1713, when it was refaced in Queen Anne style.

Under the ownership of Lieutenant-Colonel H. de Watteville in the 1920s, both the house and its garden were substantially altered by architect P. J. B. Harland, incorporating mod cons indoors, *Country Life* noted, such as a gas cooker in the kitchen and the luxury of central heating. The garden was a slender, wedge-shaped strip of land, just one room wide at its narrowest, next to the L-shaped house, but it opened out further down and covered about a third of an acre – quite a decent plot for a terraced property in the middle of town.

Outdoors, de Watteville had been exasperated by a gravel court-yard that failed to drain away water after rain. When excavations for the landscaping works were carried out, the reason was discovered: under the gravel lay the old cobbled stableyard for the inn. Harland made sense of the site by installing a modern, low-maintenance area by the house, of brick and York-stone paving, with a formal arrangement of four beds around a circular lily pond that was the home of koi carp. The pond was aligned with the view

With the dining-room doors folded back, both house and garden became one space, with the bench mirrored in the pond.

Above: *The armillary sundial on an Art Deco stone plinth designed by P. J. B. Harland, with orchard trees beyond.*

Left: *Bringing an atmosphere of country gardening into the town: a lavender-edged rose garden lay beyond the L-shaped house, around the sundial.*

from a charming dining room, formerly a dusty boot room, whose garden wall of folding doors opened out to transform it into an airy loggia.

Beyond that point the garden broadened out, and a second, four-square arrangement of flowerbeds was created within the lawns, this time around a modern stone plinth in Art Deco style, designed by the architect and topped by an armillary sphere. Palisades and a shrubbery were removed to create more openness and space; a miniature lime-tree avenue was planted to one side, shielding the garages, and on the other, a crazy-paving path was laid and edged with lavender and roses, beside a broader lawn planted with a variety of orchard trees.

Internally, the house was just as interesting, particularly its roof space, where the structural timbers of oak were found to be of exceptionally good quality, dating from 'much earlier than 1580', and with some pieces (reused from an earlier building) perhaps from as early as 1420. It was converted into an atmospheric 'studio' den, furnished with antiques and squashy sofas, with bright windows affording views of the comings and goings on the street.

That was then. In the intervening years, King's Head House has ceased to be a home; it has been converted into offices, though the structure of the house and its frontage remains much as it was in Lieutenant-Colonel de Watteville's day. The garden could not survive the same pressures on town-centre space in an expanding community. The greater part of it was walled off and sold; gone are the sundial lawn, orchard and flowerbeds, the garages and lime trees, and in their place is a car park. The house end of the garden survives, but these days the pool's uncluttered Modernism has been compromised with a central cherub fountain, and naturally planting has changed within the surrounding beds. The loggia/dining room with its folding doors has been filled in with walling and windows and now forms part of the office space.

FOUR

EASTERN COUNTIES

Great trees and imposing structures relieved the flatness of many fine gardens of the Eastern Counties. At Sudbourne Hall in Suffolk, the impressive tree collections sprang out of vast lawns, while at nearby Campsea Ashe, the cedars, yews and other massive conifers enhanced the garden's sense of enclosure and mystery. Copped Hall in Essex (*left* and *below*) used extensive masonry to give its grounds structure on a gently sloping but featureless site. The more intimate hillside garden at Mountains took a contrastingly naturalistic approach, with the emphasis on fine plants. Also in Essex, the celebrated architect Harold Peto built Classically inspired pergolas to bring grandeur and height to the level gardens of Easton Lodge. At Bawdsey Manor, on the Suffolk coast, the pergola could hardly have been more different in ambience, being an intentionally crude structure of rough stone piers and a rustically twisted roof.

COPPED HALL, ESSEX

The joy of Copped Hall a century ago was its completely over-the-top garden, designed by the stained-glass artist C. E. Kempe in the 1890s. With all the unrestrained confidence of the age – and the apparently unrestricted purse of his client – Kempe extended the house, then laid out broad, balustraded terraces on a series of levels, making the most of Copped's glorious hilltop site.

He had a head start, as much of the ground levelling had been done long ago for ornate gardens around an earlier, and larger, Elizabethan mansion, before it had all been swept away. Kempe's brief was clearly to create a setting more in keeping with the status of its owner, Ernest Wythes, the grandson of George Wythes, whose fortune had been made in the railways and new housing.

Ernest Wythes was only twenty-five years old when he began spending his (and his late elder brother's) fortunes on Copped Hall, having recently married into the aristocracy. New buildings included an improved stable block, a magnificent conservatory linked to the house by a glazed corridor, and seventeenth-century-inspired double-storey gazebos, placed at the corners of an elaborate parterre garden. In spirit and function they recall garden pavilions at Montacute in Somerset, as indeed do the obelisks springing up along the length of the balustrades. Splendid stone fountains and statues and a fine travertine-and-bronze Pan composition (see page 104) were among its elegant ornaments.

Planting was similarly lavish, maintained in 1900 by at least thirty-one gardeners. A sheltered spot under a sunny wall suited *Romneya coulteri*, a sumptuous Californian poppy with huge, white tissue-paper petals; this is a plant which will not tolerate disturbance if it is to flower, so an entire long bed was devoted purely to its breathtaking moment of glory in high summer. Roses and clematis were prodigiously spread over the terrace walls, and the generous depth of the flowerbeds enabled magnificent herbaceous borders to thrive. A 4-acre walled garden was packed with vegetables, fruits and flowers and an extensive range of glass. There were also smooth lawns, a bowling green, rose gardens and little turf stairways linking the different green levels. Tub gardening, with potted shrubs and topiarised trees, lined the walks.

The First World War changed Copped Hall. Garden staff never returned from the trenches, and the family watched from the house roof as Zeppelins coasted through the skies over London. In 1917, a disastrous fire burnt out the house; the family moved elsewhere on the estate. Ernest Wythes died in 1949 and the estate was sold in 1952. For decades, fierce battles raged over the potential of Copped as a development site, but in 1992 the Corporation of London saved the park. Copped Hall Trust bought the house and gardens in 1995 and hopes to restore a ruined and plundered site, though the expense makes restoration unlikely.

The stained-glass artist C. E. Kempe created high-maintenance gardens with gazebos placed at the corners of the elaborate parterre.

SUDBOURNE HALL, SUFFOLK

Sudbourne Hall a hundred years ago was a great estate covering more than 20 square miles and bordered on three sides by tidal rivers, occupying the low-lying land between Woodbridge, Felixstowe and Aldeburgh. Although its gardens were cultivated on an astonishing scale, it was primarily revered as a sporting estate.

When the wealthy art connoisseur Sir Richard Wallace, founder of the Wallace Collection, procured the estate in 1871, he brought to it the artistic refinements he had acquired during his privileged upbringing in Paris. Though he continued to spend most of his time in Paris, he made extensive improvements at Sudbourne. From 1872, Wallace laid out sumptuous new gardens and conservatories, terracing the area around the house, introducing broad, straight walks through the lawns, and lining the stone stairways with magnificent bronze *cinquecento* vases filled with seasonal flowers. The estate changed hands again in 1884 and in 1897, but great care and expense was still being lavished on the grounds when *Country Life*'s photographers called in 1900.

Capitalising on the horizontal nature of the landscape, a great acreage was given over to one of the largest lawns in England, trimmed by two large, steam-powered mowers – almost the last word in lawncare, though the age of the internal combustion engine was just beginning for mowing machinery. Trees grew especially well in the park, and among the finest were some ancient sycamores whose heads looked 'like the delicate-branched seaweeds of the shore'. There were also magnificent specimens of chestnuts, birches, beeches and enormous holm oaks (*Quercus ilex*), all of which displayed a luxuriance in their low-sweeping branches which had never been browsed by either cattle or deer.

But that is just the start: the flower gardens were something else again. Yellow calceolaria was mingled with brilliant-scarlet-flowered and bronze-leaved *Lobelia* 'Queen Victoria'. The same plants were also grown in a bed with the variegated-leaved and scarlet-flowered 'Mrs Pollock' pelargoniums and *Galtonia candicans*. Fibrous-rooted begonias were used very extensively in varying colours of crimson, white and pink, with purple foliage; meanwhile, scarlet-flowered tuberous begonias sprang out of a background carpet of golden Irish moss, *Spergula pilifera* aurea.

There must have been a veritable army of garden staff to keep the show going; in spring the beds were brilliant with fragrant polyanthus, violas, alyssum and spring bulbs in great variety, but particularly tulips 'of the larger kinds'. The kitchen garden would have been highly organised and productive with a plentiful range of glasshouses and vineries. Its borders, 'according to the good modern revival of an old custom', were bright with dahlias, phloxes, delphiniums, aquilegias, irises, anemones, stocks, asters and zinnias and 'fifty other varieties the modern gardener's list has such store and choice'.

Sudbourne's magnificent bronze vases came from France; beyond them lay the great lawns and fine trees that were admired for their low-sweeping branches.

Yet that is just the herbaceous areas cared for. Of course, there was more. The rose gardens at Sudbourne were just as impressive; many beds were devoted to just a single variety, be it 'La France', 'Marie Van Houtte' or the China roses – 'Cramoisie Supérieur', 'Ducher', 'Irene Watts', 'Queen Mab', 'Duke of York', 'Laurette Messimy' and others. The mixed rose beds carried further lists of the great old varieties: 'Alfred Colomb', 'Baron de Rothschild', 'Calliope', 'Captain Hayward', 'Catherine Soupert', 'Clio', 'Cécile de Chabrillant', 'Dean of Windsor' and many more.

Naturally, Sudbourne Hall had a serene lake populated by a fine range of wildfowl (when they weren't being shot), with an elegant iron bridge reaching over to an island and waterside plantations of bamboos, red-stemmed dogwoods, and pampas grasses 'in profusion and [growing] to a great size'. On the bank were 'a few of the fine pollard oaks, the peculiar product of this part of Suffolk'. Native trees – oaks, Scots pines, hazelnuts and more – were grown by the many thousands in a separate nursery ground, 'each in its square plot, and every plot in perfect health and condition', for the restocking of the estate's plantations was taken extremely seriously.

In 1909, the Sudbourne estate was purchased by Kenneth Mackenzie Clark, father of the art historian Kenneth Clark and grandfather of Alan Clark, the late politician and diarist. Mackenzie Clark was reputedly the 'man who broke the bank of Monte Carlo'. The estate became renowned in the 1920s for its breed of Sudbourne shire horses, but its years as a great sporting estate were numbered. During the Second World War, the house went into decline; it was eventually demolished in 1953 and the vast acreages broken up. At the time of going to press, the remaining 154 acres, at present a woodland nature reserve, are up for sale along with outbuildings including the gamekeeper's cottage. Planning permission to build a new house has been granted.

Above: *Sudbourne Hall, demolished in 1953, and its adjacent conservatory, built in the 1870s. The estate covered more than 20 square miles.*

Left: *An army of staff kept the floral show going to the highest standards from spring to autumn.*

BROME HALL, NORFOLK

A late-seventeenth-century Kip and Knyff drawing of Brome Hall, close to the Suffolk–Norfolk border, shows a magnificent mansion, then recently built, set in fabulous grounds with patterned parterres, plants and potted trees, beyond which stretched great avenues and deer parks.

For generations Brome Hall was the seat of the Cornwallis family, and the magazine noted, in 1898, that the photographed gardens had been created 'about fifty years ago'. Its elaborate parterres laid out in dwarf box hedging (looking threadbare in places by that time) were not appreciated by the writer; the patterns were infilled by broken tiles of blue, grey and white – this was dismissed as 'not gardening at all'.

There were ivy-smothered balustrades, pots shaped like bunched acanthus leaves, playful *putti* statuary and patterned beds of flowers cut into the lawns. A broad terrace around the south and west fronts of the house led down to another, even wider terrace where the offending parterres were laid out. Bare walls were covered with climbers and shrubs in great variety: *Ceanothus azureus*, *Akebia quinata*, jasmines – both *grandiflorum* and *nudiflorum*, fragrant wintersweet and *Magnolia grandiflora*.

The planting must have looked like a mish-mash, with copper beech and silver maples alongside flowering shrubs in great variety – laburnums, philadelphus, lilacs, spiraeas, forsythias. There were mixed borders either side of a lawned walk, and beyond were beds containing masses of hybrid perpetual roses, edged extravagantly with variegated euonymus and periwinkles. The pond was choked with water lilies. Even the kitchen garden was remarked upon for its beauty, though its contents were not disclosed. The park and its trees were also admired, particularly the fine and ancient avenues of oak on the approach drive.

A fire destroyed the magnificent sixteenth-century Brome Hall in the early nineteenth century and its replacement, a smaller house, was demolished in 1963 in favour of something even smaller and modern in design. Since the estate was broken up, only bare remnants of the Victorian gardens survive and the park has long been ploughed over.

Above: *In 1898, the parterres of Brome Hall, with their infill patterns of coloured broken tiles, were considered by critics to be 'not gardening at all'.*

Right: *The little tent among the trees gives the gardens a reassuringly human dimension beyond the sea of gravel and array of topiary.*

CAMPSEA ASHE, SUFFOLK

Captured on film in the retreating mists of an early autumn morning a century ago, Campsea Ashe's enigmatic gardens puzzled historians for decades. There were so many fascinating but disparate elements: long sections of water canal; three great avenues of limes, horse chestnuts and elms; the fabulous cedars, the immaculate elliptical bowling green; and, most intriguing of all, the strange pillows and lumpy bolsters of yew hedging.

The latter were said (in 1928) to amount to 600 yards in length, were 8 to 10 feet thick, and varied from 5 to 25 feet in height. Bearing in mind the many changes in horticultural fashion since the seventeenth century and the garden's close proximity to remodelled grounds such as Sudbourne Hall (pages 108–11) and Bawdsey Manor (pages 124–7), it was astonishing that these rare remnants of an earlier, formal age of gardening had survived so tenaciously into the twentieth century. Much less has filtered into the twenty-first.

The original 'High House' at Campsea (or Campsey) Ashe was built in 1585 by John Glover Esq., an aide to the Earl of Norfolk. It was sold in about 1700 to the Sheppard family, who gradually rebuilt a later house on the old footprint. They kept it until 1882, when the estate was bought by a son of the Earl of Lonsdale, James William Lowther (later Viscount Ullswater), who was Speaker of the House of Commons from 1905 to 1921.

Although John Glover would certainly have made a formal garden around his house, digging moats and planting avenues, the surviving traces of 'Dutch' canals and hedges appear to belong to a layout implemented by the Sheppards. Also of particular note were the many Lebanon cedars planted around the house and thought to date from at least 1750; the reasonably mild climate and loamy soil over a clay substrate seems to have suited them, for they grew luxuriantly and, like those of Lindridge in Devon, the cedars were one of the great features of the gardens.

Country Life's 1905 feature on the grounds bears the hallmarks of Gertrude Jekyll, who had already written a shorter description of the garden for a book, *Some English Gardens*. The magazine article noted the local moat-makers, still in business on many estates, cleaning and fixing these ancient water courses and restocking them with fish. There were two scenic parks, side by side: one rough and wild and full of ancient, rugged trees, where a herd of fallow deer grazed; the other smooth and set with large pollard oaks and crossed by a single line of elms. 'This park is grazed by red Suffolk cattle, Suffolk Punches, and a large flock of black horned sheep – a novel and effective grouping of park stock.' The deer park was crossed by a great avenue of four rows of limes, which ran straight up to the gardens by the house and a hundred years ago were at their peak of perfection in height and girth.

East of the house, and close to it, a long canal ran southwards for 150 yards, bordered by the quaintly sculptural yews. That they

Misty and mysterious Campsea Ashe puzzled historians for decades. The busts came from St Anne's, Lord Lonsdale's house near the Thames at Barnes.

were so strangely shaped is at least partly due to a period predating Lowther's arrival, when the hedges became neglected and smothered with ivy. By 1905, it had taken Lowther 'fifteen years to eradicate the ivy and repair the mischief'.

On one side of the canal lay parkland, and on the other a red-brick walled garden – formerly used for raising fruit and vegetables – with a parallel canal beyond the opposite wall. Lady Ullswater converted most of the walled grounds into flower gardens; an article written by her husband in 1928 for the *Royal Horticultural Society Journal* describes them in detail.

A central gravel path was lined with 60 yards of vivid red-and-white borders, edged with 'Shrubland Pet' pelargonium and 'Sutton's Scarlet' verbena. The blue border – edged by nemophila and the dwarf 'Butterfly' delphinium – included nigella, commelina, blue salvias in variety, anchusas and much else besides. There was an equally sumptuous mauve border, and another featuring late summer's yellow flowers in great variety. South of the walled garden was a formal garden devoted to sweetly fragrant heliotropes, with standards of 'Mme de Bussy' rising out of bushes of 'Lady Minto' and 'Mrs J. W. Lowther' – varieties which seem to have been consigned to history. Among Lord Ullswater's enthu-

siasms were the specimen trees and flowering shrubs, and a 'Japanese' garden.

The fine bowling green was aligned on an ancient east–west axis through the centre of the house front. In all probability it dates from John Glover's time, such conceits being coveted status symbols of the early seventeenth century. (The much-admired Chelsea garden of Sir John Danvers, begun in around 1622, contained a large tree-lined oval of grass created for the fashionable pastime of bowling.)

When Lord Ullswater died, in 1949, the 2,350-acre Campsea Ashe estate was bought by the Desborough Settlement Trust as part of a tax-saving measure. But this was not a rescue mission; on Lady Desborough's death in 1953 it was sold again. At around this time the house was demolished and its estate broken up; consequently, most of the gardens have completely disappeared, and though some of the park remains, much was ploughed up for crops.

Right: *The mysterious yew topiaries that surrounded the oval bowling green, seen here from one of the long canals in an unpublished photograph.*

Below: *Another unpublished photograph of the bowling green, aligned on the house front. Campsea Ashe's cedars were famously handsome.*

MOUNTAINS, ESSEX

Mountains, on a hillside site near Maldon in Essex, was the dower house of Braxted Park and became the home of Lady Du Cane and her two daughters in the last decade of the nineteenth century. Around 2½ acres of Mountains' approximately 50-acre domain were intensively gardened, with spring and early summer erupting in magnificent displays of bulbs and blossoms around a broad lawn dotted with apple trees. By the mid-1920s, when *Country Life*'s photographs were taken, it was a mature landscape artistically laid out in a collection of painterly views, with plenty of species that would have been of interest to the plantsman.

The original eighteenth-century brick farmhouse overlooked a valley on the west side which was watered by a spring-fed brook arising in the grounds. Far-reaching views to the south and south-east took in the estuary of the River Blackwater, with its Osea Island and the misty blues and greens of the flatlands beyond.

Left: Azaleas, rhododendrons and acers in an unpublished view of the Japanese garden, a distillation of the Du Cane sisters' travels in Japan.

Below: A view along the borders up to the summerhouse. Its roof was made by one of the last of a family of traditional Suffolk thatchers.

The wooded dell was laid out as a rock garden and Japanese garden, and the outer reaches were maintained with a suitably wildish ambience. 'Lady du Cane has had the good judgment not to push the requirements of a rock garden too far, so that the nature of the combe is still predominant,' observed Christopher Hussey in 1925. Oddly, though, he did not mention the Japanese garden, nor choose to publish a photograph of it, though the Japanese connection is a vital part of the story.

At the start of the twentieth century, Lady Du Cane's unconventional daughters, Ella and Florence, travelled overseas extensively, and unchaperoned, painting what they saw and making copious notes. The result of one of their expeditions was an exquisite little book, *The Flowers and Gardens of Japan*, which was written by Florence and illustrated by Ella. It became a bestseller and was reprinted several times; the evocative watercolours of tea-houses and cherry blossoms, potted peonies at the waterside, and geishas among trailing wisterias had universal appeal.

So the Japanese garden at Mountains had special significance and indeed it was furnished with both ornaments and plants brought back from the daughters' travels. Moist soil at the water's edge provided a home for swathes of *Iris ensata* in a multitude of hues;

they had been brought back from the then-famous Hori-Kiri gardens of Tokyo. The sight of the streamside irises each summer must have rekindled the Du Cane girls' memories of the 'dew month' at Hori-Kiri, when paths winding through the rice fields on the banks of the Sumida River were crowded with sightseers, 'all bent in one direction and with the same intent' – to see the brief flowering of the irises. 'Some seventy varieties of this king of irises are grown,' Florence wrote in *The Flowers and Gardens of Japan*, 'many raised from seed and jealously treasured by the owner … . Some are pure white, only veined with a faint tinge of green; some have a margin of lilac; some are shaded; some mottled; but surely the most beautiful of all is just a great single bloom of one shade, be it white, lilac, or blue.'

On the wildish slopes of the lower garden were rampant fountains of *wichuraiana* roses, trailing over the grass and merging with broom and gorse in the gravelly soil. Nearby, swagged festoons of cerise Rosa 'Papa Gontier' bloomed beside a rainbow wave of tall bearded irises in a clutch of old-fashioned varieties that are now either rare or extinct. Footpaths snaked through the shrubberies, and on the east side a daffodil-speckled lawn was also bright with cherry trees and Japanese maples.

A substantial wing was added to the house in the early 1920s and a fashionable crazy-paving terrace was set out beside it, leading eastwards to a charming summerhouse roofed by a Suffolk thatcher, one of the last practitioners of the craft for which his family had long been famous. Flowerbeds carved out of the terrace and along a stretch of garden wall were densely planted with daring blocks of boldly contrasting tulips: dramatically blackish-purple 'Faust' and 'Tulipe Noire'; primrose-yellow 'Ellen Willmott'; candy-pink 'Clara Butt'; flame-coloured 'Orange King'. Tubs near the house were packed with large agapanthus for summer. The tulip theme also flourished in a pair of pastel-hued borders running south from the summerhouse. Here their spring displays of carmine, pink and white tulips sprang out from mats of aubrieta, among scented wallflowers and delicate pink saxifrage. From June, these borders and the beds around the house wore the classic soft pinks, whites and blues of peonies, campanulas, delphiniums, arum lilies and *Iris pallida*.

Today, although Mountains survives as a private house with a pretty garden, it is not the lavish Du Cane garden tended by several staff and planted with the artistic verve of those intrepid sisters. The orchard trees and the intensively cultivated borders are gone, the terraces have been relaid, and a new pattern of formal beds near the house has recently been laid out. The most tenacious survivor has been the Japanese dell, which, though unquestionably altered, still boasts magnificent displays of candelabra primulas, a few of the Hori-Kiri irises – and a not-so-welcome legacy of the sisters' plant imports: the invincible Japanese knotweed.

Looking along the double border from the summerhouse. Abundant tulips and a Clematis montana *were joined by the orchard's apple blossoms.*

EASTON LODGE, ESSEX

In a county not short of glamorous, high-budget gardens, palatial Easton Lodge in its 1,000-acre park had the most romantic provenance, being the home (and for a while the royal love nest) of the Countess of Warwick. The beautiful countess, known as Daisy, was born in 1861 and had inherited a great fortune – 14,000 acres of estates, coal mines, quarries and personal income equivalent to one million pounds a year in today's money – at the tender age of four.

Having married Lord Brooke in 1881, she spent princely sums on her house and gardens, particularly as they were the scene of lavish and regular entertaining for the Prince of Wales and his entourage (for some years she was the mistress whom the Prince called 'my darling Daisy wife'). In the 1890s, she created sentimental but undistinguished enclosed gardens, including a 'Garden of Friendship' with concentric circles of beds containing plants donated by friends; an area called 'The Border of Sentiment' contained many planted by the Prince himself.

In 1895, Daisy converted to socialism and filled her time with worthy causes, in the process losing the Prince's ardour, but her passion for her garden grew, and in 1903 Harold Peto created a number of dramatic set-pieces in the grounds. Peto's work, north of the house, led from flower-studded lawns to a rolled tennis and croquet lawn, bordered on two sides by arched pergola walks of fine *treillage* wreathed in climbing vines, clematis and roses. From there steps led into a paved sunken garden with a huge water-lily pool enclosed by balustrades, fashioned in Ham Hill stone brought from Somerset, beyond which were tree-lined walks, a maze and a Japanese tea-house by the lake. Today, alas, after years of partial restorations following decades of decline, Easton Lodge seems doomed by the expanding Stansted International Airport that is most unfortunately right on its doorstep.

Above: *The Japanese tea-house, designed by Harold Peto.*

Right: *Peto's great arched pergolas were erected on either side of a tennis lawn. Netting fixed on the roofs provided good anchorage for climbing roses and vines.*

BAWDSEY MANOR, SUFFOLK

Rock gardens were at the height of fashion when Bawdsey Manor's cliffscape was featured by *Country Life* in 1909. Reginald Farrer's book *My Rock Garden* had become a bestseller, as indeed had Gertrude Jekyll's *Wall and Water Gardens* (first published by *Country Life* in 1901), which had a good deal to say about planting in tricky places. Sir Frank Crisp's magnificently eclectic rock garden at Friar Park, Henley, complete with its 30-foot miniature Matterhorn and tumbling waterfalls, was being praised (though not by Farrer) as a 'paradise of alpine flowers', and few garden owners could call their grounds complete without at least one piece of stony moraine tucked away somewhere.

But at Bawdsey Manor, the setting for a 'rock' garden was unique. In medieval times, Bawdsey had been an island reached by a causeway and belonged to the Kingshaven, a cluster of harbours around the mouth of the River Deben. Gradually the Deben silted up and changed course, the sea cut its way farther in, and Bawdsey became a high and dry part of the Suffolk coastline.

Sir Cuthbert Quilter, the wealthy MP for Ipswich (and father of the composer Roger Quilter) who had made his fortune in stockbroking and business, was renting Hintlesham Hall when he spotted the Bawdsey peninsula while out shooting as a guest of Lord Rendlesham. It was remote and virtually inaccessible by road, with tracts of land exhausted from mining coprolites – fossilised dung of aquatic creatures in the shelly crag soils – which yielded phosphates for agricultural fertilisers.

Nevertheless, Quilter bought at auction several hundred acres and the manorship of Bawdsey, with its lonely Martello tower and cluster of lifeboat huts, and decided to make it his eventual home, though it began more modestly as a seaside retreat.

Fancifully romantic blood must have coursed through the otherwise astute Quilter veins for him to choose such a raw, inaccessible spot, with its big skies and shimmering reeds. (However, the wildfowl shooting was prodigious, as we can see from the game records of nearby Sudbourne Hall.) The only feasible access to Bawdsey

Above: The pergola pathway to the sea, one of several unpublished photographs of the rockworks carried out by James Pulham & Son.

Left: A tiered system of rockwork and terraces on the cliff face became home to self-sowers including red valerian and Lupinus arboreus.

was by boat from Felixstowe, yet before long a new house was built, albeit in piecemeal form and in an eclectic range of styles.

Likewise, the gardens embraced a variety of influences; first, though, hundreds of trees were planted along the clifftop to provide a belt of shelter from salt-laden winds blowing in off the North Sea. From the staircase hall of the central block of the house there was access to a garden room, where large glass windows illuminated mimosa trees and doors opened on to a south-facing terrace. The terrace led down to another, which featured at one end a Jacobean-style tea-house, the interior of which was gaily lined with coloured tiles from southern Italy. A magnificent 2-acre kitchen garden was built, surrounded by high brick walls with delicately carved stone pediments set over elaborate wrought-iron gateways. Extensive glasshouses lined two of the walls; a flagstone main path, flanked by sumptuous herbaceous borders, led to a handsome Classical orangery, modelled on one at Hintlesham Hall which the Quilters had admired during their ten-year tenancy there.

The round Martello tower, an artillery relic of the sea defences built on this coastline during the Napoleonic Wars, was not in line with Lady Quilter's view of what constituted an acceptable garden folly, and it was demolished with gunpowder. Yet its footprint, once the rubble was removed, provided the template for a perfect circular garden of flowers and roses, and the material from the demolitions was put to good use in creating artificial tunnels giving access to the quarter-mile of cliff terraces that were unique to Bawdsey. A zigzagging network of footpaths and steps was cut into the rock face leading down to the beach, and naturally the works were carried out by the famously skilful rockwork specialists, James Pulham & Son. The cliff-walk plants were species that could withstand the demanding conditions of stony crevices lacking any nourishment: pink thrift, pale-yellow *Lupinus arboreus*, erigerons, sea hollies and *Centranthus ruber*. At the top of the cliff, a pergola straddled an enticing path offering a window view of the sea, its quaint rustic roof garlanded with climbing roses. With gradual acquisitions of land, the Quilters' estate eventually comprised 10,000 acres, wherein over two million trees were planted and most of Bawdsey village was rebuilt, for the Quilters were extensively staffed and thus injected new life and money into a formerly dwindling community.

In 1935, Bawdsey Manor was selected as the site for a new research station where the Royal Air Force could develop radio direction-finding radar, which they did successfully, just in time for the Second World War. For some years afterwards it remained an RAF research station. The Quilters' house survives, but these days it is a residential college and very little of the garden remains, though skeleton walls and paths hint at its former grandeur; the cliff walks are inaccessible, enshrouded with shrubberies of tamarisk and still fenced off by military barbed wire.

When a Martello tower was blown up with gunpowder, its circular footprint was made into a garden; its rubble was used in the cliff-garden tunnels.

FIVE

EAST MIDLANDS

For some great estates of the East Midlands, close proximity to the industrial heartland was their downfall.
Thus Drakelowe Hall, at Burton-on-Trent, disappeared altogether, while Clumber Park, near Nottingham, became a valuable recreational
space for the public once its house had been demolished and the land sold off. The hunting estate of Papillon Hall (*left* and *below*)
included Edwin Lutyens' least known but most consummately lost garden, which appears to have been doomed by forces beyond the
obviously practical ones that sealed the fate of many lost houses. Time has been kinder to Castle Ashby, which is still a fine estate: its great
terraces cling on, albeit with easily managed lawns and sparse flowerbeds, replacing the prohibitively high-maintenance parterres.
Plant collections are always the most vulnerable to loss; at Caunton Manor, Reynolds Hole's vast collection of
roses did not last beyond his own long lifetime.

PAPILLON HALL, LEICESTERSHIRE

Most of Edwin Lutyens' major houses and gardens have survived down the years but Papillon Hall is a curious exception. It was commissioned in 1903 by Captain Frank Ashton Bellville, who had inherited a fortune made from Keen's mustard. It was the hunting that brought Bellville to the area, but his desire to enlarge the house may have been on account of its mysterious history.

Papillon Hall had changed hands many times over the previous two centuries and there was a persistent local rumour that the place was haunted, backed up by the existence of a pair of early-eighteenth-century slippers locked in a tiny cupboard, the removal of which, according to the title deeds, was not permitted or ill fate would befall the owner of the house.

Lutyens picked up the property's name, creating a house in butterfly plan around the core of the seventeenth-century octagonal stone mansion. New wings were splayed out from the four corners

of the old house with circulation and service spaces neatly incorporated. These rare photographs of Papillon Hall, dating from late summer 1911, display classic Lutyens features of the period: millstones in the pavings; stairways based on sections of a circle; steps built up with tiles and topped with sawn stone; flagstone paths cutting gracefully through planes of turf. His conjuring tricks with hard and soft materials both control and delight the eye.

Generous terraces filled out the spaces between the butterfly wings to the east and south; the latter was a broiling suntrap, cooled by the presence of a water-lily pool with central fountain. The surrounding beds were planted with roses and seasonal bedding. Wall climbers included roses and the large-leaved vine *Vitis coignetiae*. Broad lawns and further gardens, including herbaceous borders, and a charming walk to a summerhouse could be reached via steps that led down from a path encircling most of the house. The west side formed the entrance, leading to a serenely Classical court: enclosed, uncluttered and open to the sky.

Bellville died in 1937 and the house was occupied by American troops during the Second World War. No buyer could be found after the War and this unlucky house was demolished in 1950, though tattered remnants of Lutyens' garden still lie in the fields.

Left: Lutyens brought the flower gardens right up to the house, seen here on the east side.

Above: The walk to the summerhouse, incorporating views of the Leicestershire countryside beyond the gate piers.

CASTLE ASHBY, NORTHAMPTONSHIRE

Castle Ashby (the hamlet in the ash trees) is a handsome house of golden Northamptonshire limestone set within a 200-acre park on the Marquess of Northampton's 10,000-acre estate. When Capability Brown worked on the grounds during the 1760s, he deformalised a medieval park crossed by four very long, straight avenues planted in the seventeenth century. One of them, stretching out for 3 miles to the south, was left intact, while the others were largely abolished or incorporated into looser clumps of trees. He also enlarged pools from an earlier design to make two informal lakes, known as Park Pond and Menagerie Pond, added an Ionic temple with menagerie overlooking the latter, and built a dairy with a Classical façade near the house. Elizabethan formal gardens extending down the eastern vista were entirely swept away.

The next radical reconstruction came exactly a century later, when the 3rd Marquess of Northampton decided to put formality back into the east side and engaged Sir Digby Wyatt to help him make alterations. They created a fashionably lively parterre garden of terraces enclosed by balustrades; to the south-east a series of handsome glasshouses was built by Wyatt, surrounded by an 'Italian' garden of straight walks and box-edged beds of roses and carnations. Beyond these a high wall with fine gateways was erected around the huge, rectangular kitchen garden.

When Charles Latham photographed the great parterres in 1897, he captured a deliciously high-maintenance confection: a sequence of embroidery patterns that went even further than Nesfield's classic set-pieces of the period. The Marquess himself is credited with their design. Two parterres, the chief of which can be seen in the photograph, were laid out in brilliantly executed compositions that included the family's initials and heraldic devices and stylised flower motifs, carefully arranged in blocks of colourful bedding plants, including white and purple strains of verbena, scarlet pelargoniums and blue lobelia.

Even Gertrude Jekyll, not usually a fan of formal Victoriana, admired the arrangement, writing in *Garden Ornament* (1918): 'Beautiful examples of the good treatment of parterres existed a few years ago at Castle Ashby, and it is to be hoped that the same tradition is maintained. They were delightfully planned for colour harmony, so that each department formed a satisfying picture. ... the best possible utilisation of the bedding system, which, in these large parterres, was, and always is, absolutely in place.'

They could not be maintained at that rate, of course, and today's parterres are greatly simplified with much of the detailed pattern grassed over. One attractive survivor, however, is the carved stone balustrade enclosing the parterres, which reads: 'Consider the lilies of the field, how they grow; they toil not, neither do they spin; and yet I say unto you that even Solomon in all his glory was not arrayed like one of these.'

White and purple verbena, scarlet pelargoniums and blue lobelias were among the summer flowers chosen to fill out the great parterres, photographed in 1897.

CLUMBER PARK, NOTTINGHAMSHIRE

A lone boatman sculls across the 200-acre lake beside the house at Clumber Park in one of *Country Life*'s most evocative sets of photographs. Substitute the rowboat for a gondola and the scene would immediately suggest a Venetian palace, with the stairs of its great terrace descending into the lapping water where our boatman may alight to pick up passengers. The story of Clumber involves a flush of English dukes, but the connections with Italy are not entirely fanciful; at least one of Clumber's heirs was cheated out of a fortune by thieves while savouring the Italian tranche of the Grand Tour, as Casanova recorded in his memoirs.

But for all its evocations of the Veneto, the Clumber Estate lies on the edge of Sherwood Forest, where some 4,000 acres were enclosed by Thomas Pelham Holles, 1st Duke of Newcastle-under-Lyme (who was also, rather confusingly, 4th Duke of Newcastle-

upon-Tyne) in 1707. From the early eighteenth century, the new boundary described a circuit of 13 miles but it remained without a house until the Duke's nephew, Henry Fiennes Clinton (the 2nd Duke), built one designed by Stephen Wright at the close of the 1760s. Prior to that the land was unprepossessingly described as 'little more than a black heath full of rabbits, having a narrow river running through it, with a small boggy close or two'. Probably for some while it had only been used for hunting, but the slender stretch of river gave it the potential, in the right hands, to become a magnificent setting.

Capability Brown was brought in to landscape the park and worked at Clumber between 1774 and 1789, at a cost of £6,612. Brown dammed the River Poulter at two points so that, although the lake was shallow, its plentiful supply of water produced a generous-looking result. Throsby's updated edition of Thoroton's *History of Nottinghamshire* (1797) noted that 'from the new bridge which spans the apparent endless stream which waters Clumber there appears an harmonious whole of grandeur'.

But the 2nd Duke died in 1794 and his son passed away the following year, so that the 4th Duke inherited at the age of ten.

Left: The south-facing terraces between the house and the lake. Flowerbeds were volcanoes of colour, edged by dwarf bedding plants.

Below: Beyond the majestic terraces, Clumber's maturing trees became a feature of the park. Bodley's chapel spire looms above them on the left.

As a young man visiting France at the wrong moment, Henry Pelham Fiennes Pelham Clinton was detained by Napoleon's régime for four years, but upon his return to Nottinghamshire in 1807, he soon married the daughter of a coal baron who brought with her a considerable fortune. Aided by this largesse, in 1839 the 4th Duke bought the nearby Worksop Manor estate from the Duke of Norfolk and promptly demolished a Classical palace by James Paine, which, though impressive, had never been fully completed. Worksop's elegant garden ornaments and structures were carted back to Clumber to grace the magnificent terraces leading up to the water's edge designed by William Sawrey Gilpin.

When it was the turn of the 5th Duke, who inherited aged forty in 1851, plans were made for further modifications, not least, perhaps, to bring a new broom into his father's house; their political views had differed widely and had caused many rifts. Charles Barry, architect of the Houses of Parliament, prepared plans for house and garden alterations at Clumber in 1857, including designs for elaborate parterres to east and west. These were not carried out, however, and the 5th Duke, worn out by work at the War Office, died suddenly at Clumber in his fifty-third year.

Although its park was by now a magnificent and serene prospect with maturing cedars of Lebanon and Turkey oaks and a splendid 3-mile avenue of young and flourishing lime trees, Clumber was to undergo further calamities. The 6th Duke, Henry Pelham Alexander Pelham-Clinton, was 'a very noted sportsman in his day, but of expensive habits', so that he left the estates encumbered when he died in February 1879. Worse was to come. A month later the house was in flames. The old entrance and staircase, two or three sitting rooms and many bedrooms were destroyed, while the lawns and terraces 'were strewn with hastily removed valuables, which were soon half buried in the falling snow'.

So, once again, a young heir – then aged only fifteen – inherited unfortunate Clumber. Charles Barry Junior, Sir Charles's son, rebuilt the house on an immensely grand scale after the fire with work beginning in June 1880. A magnificent private chapel, larger than many parish churches, was built beside the terraces by the architect G. F. Bodley. The photographs of 1908 show a confident Clumber, expensively planted with bedded-out flowers around a glorious composition of fountains and urns, with a parade of stone cranes watching over the waters from the balustrade. 'Set in the midst of its glorious sylvan surroundings, it is a splendid and desirable home,' declared *Country Life*, but evidently the 7th Duke thought otherwise – he moved out the same year.

The house, too expensive to maintain, was demolished in 1938 by the next generation and the gardens disappeared. The outbreak of the Second World War thwarted plans to build a new house, and the estate was sold in 1948 to the National Trust, which maintains what is left as a scenic and much-loved park for the region.

In its heyday, the Lincoln Terrace, designed by William Sawrey Gilpin, was a romantic lakeside walk ornamented with a parade of urns and flowers.

DRAKELOWE HALL, DERBYSHIRE

The manor of Drakelowe belonged to one family in an unbroken line through twenty-eight generations, which made its complete destruction all the more tragic. For several hundred years prior to the Industrial Revolution, the setting of the house must have been idyllic without being remote. Occupying lowland beside the River Trent, this was an area of lushly fertile woods and meadows near a stretch of the great Roman thoroughfare of Ryknild Street.

The family could be traced back to Ralph de Toeni, the standard-bearer of William the Conqueror at the Battle of Hastings. Later, William of Stafford founded the Augustinian priory at Gresley and the family subsequently took up the name of Gresley, which continued down the centuries. By the time that *Country Life* visited Drakelowe in 1902 and again in 1907, it was the seat of Sir Robert Gresley, 11th Baronet, whose father had died in 1868 when he was just two years old.

The creeper-clad house was a handsome Tudor and Jacobean edifice, with crenellated walls and barley-twist chimneys built on to more ancient structures, but Sir Robert Gresley declared: 'It is the pleasure grounds and gardens which are the chief beauty of the place, many of the hollies and yews lining the walks being well over 30 feet in height.' This remark suggests a feeling for Picturesque landscape, which may account for the survival of Drakelowe's extraordinary Painted Dining Room, of which more later.

A century ago, Drakelowe Hall was approached by a magnificent mile-long avenue of mature elms, planted in double rows. The 580-acre park was noted for the great stature of the oak and beech trees among the extensive woods, and they must have provided much-needed sanctuary from an ever-encroaching industrial landscape of coal mines, smoky potteries, limestone excavations and yeasty air clouding out of the great breweries of nearby Burton-upon-Trent.

From a balustraded terrace along one side of the house you could descend fine stairways to terraced lawns and a bastioned embankment lapped by the waters of the Trent, a successful set-piece designed by F. Inigo Thomas in 1902.

Ornamental gardens, enclosed by the high brick walls that probably also sheltered the kitchen grounds, were reached through handsome stone entrances hung with wrought-iron gates. The brickwork was garlanded with climbers – assorted clematis, roses and ornamental vines.

The Circle Garden must have been particularly peaceful, reached by the deep shade of vine-engulfed tunnels, enclosed by tall evergreens and with the sound of water trickling from a shell held aloft by a lead mermaid fountain in its circular pool. Another route in the walled gardens reached a smaller stone basin, forming the cross-axis of four grass walks, one of them leading past peony borders and another running between herbaceous beds.

The walled gardens were a sequence of secretive enclosures hidden by tall trees, but beyond them the scene opened out on to the waters of the River Trent.

Then there was the long rose walk, where summer fragrances would be trapped, on one side by a high brick wall decked in vines and roses, and on the other by tall shrubberies and a narrow herbaceous border. Up the centre ran a series of small beds of roses, edged by dwarf box.

One of the great features of Drakelowe was a rare 'indoor garden' entirely covering the dining-room interior. It had been painted by Paul Sandby (1730–1809), a member of the Royal Academy and often described as 'the father of the English watercolour'. It had been recently completed when Miss Anna Seward of Lichfield observed in 1794: 'Sir Nigel hath adorned one of his rooms with singular happiness. It is large, one side painted with forest scenery, whose majestic trees arch over the coved ceiling. Through them we see glades, tufted banks and ascending walks in perspective. The opposite side of the room exhibits a Peak valley, the front shows a prospect of more distant country, vieing with the beauties of the real one, admitted opposite through a crystal wall of window. Its chimney-piece, formed of spars and ores and shells, represents a grotto. Real pales, painted green and breast high, are placed a few

inches from the walls and increase the power of the deception.' *Country Life*'s Edwardian authors were less enthusiastic, declaring it 'not in accord with the taste of these days' in 1902, while in 1907 it was dismissed as an example of 'the depraved taste of the late eighteenth century'.

Though the Gresleys' occupation of Drakelowe had been exceptionally long, change was nigh, both indoors and out. Like so many fine estates, it became too expensive to retain in the twentieth century. The house and 707 acres were sold in 1933, the contents having already gone. The house was demolished in 1938, and in 1948 the land was compulsorily acquired for a huge coal-fired power station, which has entirely smothered the scenic grounds. Part of the Painted Dining Room was rescued, however, and conveyed to the Victoria and Albert Museum, where it remains.

Above: *The Circle Garden created a world apart from the encroaching industrial landscape of coal mines and smoky potteries.*

Right: *The central feature of the Circle Garden: its mermaid fountain pool, enclosed by rings of turf and gravelled paths.*

CAUNTON MANOR, NOTTINGHAMSHIRE

Six miles north-west of Newark, near a stream that feeds into the great meanders of the Trent, Caunton Manor sits secure and square within its demesne. The early-eighteenth-century house played a key part in the history of a very English love of roses.

It was the family home of Samuel Reynolds Hole (1819–1904), Canon of Lincoln and later Dean of Rochester, a keen sportsman and witty raconteur renowned for the excellence of his sermons and speeches, for which he used no notes. But this hunting squire, who was in all respects larger than life, is famous among gardeners for his bestselling books on roses and for being the first president of the Royal National Rose Society.

At Caunton, his passion for roses was ignited one summer's evening in 1846, when he was relaxing in the garden with book and cigar. His eyes 'rested on a rose' – the rich crimson gallica 'd'Aguesseau' – and he became 'overpowered by the conviction that the rose was the loveliest of all the flowers'. From that moment the gardens at Caunton began to burgeon with roses, the numbers increasing to 100, then 1,000, and ultimately 5,000, even extending into the home farm, whereupon Reynolds Hole's father expressed a hope that he would leave a *little* space for the wheat.

The walled kitchen garden became overrun by roses destined for the fierce rivalry of the show bench. Roses filled island beds and curved borders skirting the broad and level lawns. Ramblers 'Ayrshire', 'Aimée Vibert' and 'Lamarque' romped up high walls, as did the delicate 'Banksians' in white and primrose-yellow. Tea roses and hybrid perpetuals were experimentally planted against walls and trained up poles, where, the good clergyman noted, they 'will develop a surprising vigour'; shrub roses bordered the scenic and shady walks through the Wild Garden. It was not *all* roses, however. There were fine cedars and other specimen conifers on the broad lawns; Mrs Hole grew many herbaceous flowers and a fernery was cultivated in a wooded glade.

In December 1887, Reynolds Hole was made Dean of Rochester, a promotion which sadly forced him to uproot his family – and as many of the roses as he could manage – to settle in Kent. The garden began to be dismantled; the following May his wife Caroline organised a sale of plants (including many roses), books, horses, carriages and livestock at Caunton. Although the dean returned whenever he was able to, the prodigious amount of work to which he committed himself made visits back home infrequent.

Reynolds Hole was photographed by *Country Life* at Caunton in 1899. Then in his eightieth year, his valedictory article of 21 October 1899 regrets the disappearance of his favourite flowers, the 5,000 varieties by then reduced to 500. After more than fifty years among roses, 'Gloire de Dijon' remained his all-time favourite, followed by 'La France', 'Mrs Laing' and 'Marie Van Houtte'.

A rare photograph of Samuel Reynolds Hole in his eightieth year, during a return visit to Caunton. He regretted the reduced quantity of roses in the gardens.

SIX

WEST MIDLANDS

Of all the lost gardens in *Country Life*'s archive, those in the West Midlands – largely built on wealth derived from new industries –
convey a very Victorian preoccupation with spending power and the need to show it off. The ruins of Lilleshall Abbey (*left*)
were a distant eye-catcher to be seen from the hall, beyond its seasonal flowerbeds and manicured terraced walks. Enville Hall boasted a
fabulously exotic conservatory and fountains to rival those at Chatsworth; Hewell Grange had its rock gardens (*below*) as well as
an inconceivably ornate 'French' garden laid out in front of the new house. The formal garden at Hoar Cross demanded many skilled hands
for its upkeep, while the windows of Stoke Edith looked on to highly wrought Nesfield parterres in dwarf box, their patterns pencilled
in with expensive coloured gravels. Only Cleeve Prior bucks the trend, with the old manor's haunting, ancient yews
bringing mystery into the hard-working farmyard.

ENVILLE HALL, STAFFORDSHIRE

Even with so much water to hand in elegant pools around the park, when Enville Hall caught fire in November 1904, very little could be done to save its central portion, for ice had frozen over the ponds. A housekeeper had discovered the blaze and the estate workers did the best they could to fight the flames while a cyclist pedalled to nearby Stourbridge to rouse the fire brigade. Though most of the contents were saved, there was considerable smoke damage to the building.

Refurbishments began almost immediately, however, and by 1907 the ruined central section had been restored. But if there had been no belt-tightening in the management of the Hall and its grounds prior to this event or immediately after it (and the photographs certainly indicate lavish spending on the gardens in 1901), changes of fortune would arrive with the First World War.

Less than four years prior to the fire, *Country Life* had paid tribute to Enville, the home of Catherine, Countess of Stamford and Warrington, in a lengthy feature whose photographs captured a magnificent, showy garden, still being maintained to rigorous high-Victorian standards by a large team of skilled staff.

During the lifetime of the energetic 7th Earl of Stamford, the Enville estate was enlarged, and it was he who remodelled the existing gardens after 1845, creating a style that persisted at Enville through the rest of the nineteenth century. The Great Flower Lawn was a vast area of level turf with many circular beds cut out of it to form domes of bedded-out flowers. Standard roses and wide-bowled vases of flowers were positioned in pairs at evenly spaced intervals beside the neat gravel paths snaking through the lawns. One area was devoted to an ornate rose garden with a trim pattern of beds edged in dwarf box, centred upon a pretty wirework

Above: *The serene Shell Fountain and, beyond, the great park with its open green expanses, deliberately contrasting with gloomier walks among the trees.*

Left: *Enville's great conservatory seemed to rival the Crystal Palace. It was a triumphant expression of the local glass and iron industries.*

147

gazebo. Then there was the Long Walk, a feature that enjoyed special renown: a straight footpath led for over 150 yards past ribbon borders of bedded-out flowers, arranged in ascending tiers from front to back, in stripes of contrasting colours. Ribbon borders were much in vogue in the 1850s, and in Midlands gardens particularly (the gardener George Fleming had made them famous at Trentham Hall); those at Enville were especially fine, composed of up to eight different strands of colour on each side, rather than the more usual, and economical, three. Appropriate subjects for this treatment included popular long-season bedding plants such as pelargoniums, scarlet lobelia, dark-leaved perilla, begonias, hollyhocks and also standard roses.

Water was used in multifarious ways to ornament the grounds through a variety of lakes, limpid ponds and cleverly wrought fountains. Taking up the gauntlet thrown down by Paxton at Chatsworth, Derbyshire, where he had created a magnificent Emperor Fountain sending up a jet of water that could reach 180 feet into the air (by gravity alone), Enville was to have its own, pump-driven version. Enville's fountains were many and varied, including the Sea-horse Lake, with its arrangement of Neptune amid a gathering of fishtailed horses frolicking among numerous water jets, and the Dolphin Fountain, a large, elaborate sculpture rising out of a circular pool. The Willow Lake was a serene boating pond edged with weeping willows, and the Shell Fountain provided yet another elegant pool, drizzling water seductively from the curves of its central 'shell'.

But of all its garden features, by far the most magnificent was Enville's great conservatory. Built by Gray and Ormson in 1853–55 on a scale not far short of the famous Crystal Palace created for the Great Exhibition of 1851, Enville's steamy hothouse of palms and other exotica was a fantastical conceit in glass and wrought iron, with timber glazing bars. From its onion-topped domes suggestive of Brighton Pavilion down to the Gothic arches and pinnacled corners of its main frame, it was for nearly seventy years one of the great private wonders of the horticultural world.

Yet there were also earlier and subtler strands of interest to be savoured at Enville, in the work that had been carried out for the 4th and 5th Earls of Stamford. The beauty of its great park was attributed to the partial involvement of William Shenstone (1714–63), a poet and landscape theorist whose own garden, The Leasowes (local vernacular for 'the meadows'), was nearby. His small park was a celebrated *ferme ornée*, which, even after his death,

was a place of pilgrimage for anyone eager to be moved by feelings of grandeur, beauty, variety and melancholy as they progressed through its prescribed route (though not for William Gilpin, who felt Shenstone had 'done too much' and spoilt the effect). 'Gardening may be divided into three species – kitchen-gardening – parterre gardening – and landskip, or picturesque gardening,' wrote Shenstone. As a poet, it was the latter 'species', of course, that consumed his interest.

At Enville, the Picturesque landscape includes walks among woods and pools, the open green expanses and contrastingly thick and gloomy umbrage among the dark yews. A cascade, 'which pours over the rocks in a deep glen, whose broken sides are thickly vested with laurel and other shrubs', was believed to be Shenstone's work. Among the little buildings scattered through the grounds, there was a 'handsome rotunda, overshadowed by a bold and lofty wood', a mid-seventeenth-century Gothic-arched greenhouse by Sanderson Miller, a hermit's house and a Chinese temple. Upon Shenstone's death, a small chapel in a remote part of the estate was dedicated to him by the 4th Earl.

Enville Hall and its 6,500-acre estate are still owned by the same family, having come down through the female line; however, much has changed in the grounds. Few of the gardeners returned from the trenches of the Great War and therefore labour-saving measures were needed; the ribbon borders and most of the ornate flowerbeds disappeared and the waterworks ceased to function. In the 1920s, the glass was removed from the great conservatory, which could no longer be heated due to the huge quantities of coal required to feed its hungry boilers every day. It lasted as a whale-like skeleton until the 1950s, when the iron frame was also dismantled.

Other presently 'lost' items should experience a happier fate. Much of the eighteenth-century landscape is currently overgrown, with little buildings engulfed in trees and undergrowth, but a ten-year restoration project has just begun which will restore the cascade and woodland walks, but not the Victoriana.

Above: *Enville's ribbon borders were famously elaborate, with as many as eight rows per side, strictly graded in colour and ascending height.*

Right: *Rosarians cultivating their roses for the show bench popularised a bare-earth, monoculture approach, magnificently demonstrated at Enville.*

HEWELL GRANGE, WORCESTERSHIRE

Looking at the splendour of Hewell Grange as photographed a century ago, with its intricate confection of gardens linked by scores of trimmed arches and avenues, it appears a work of incredible ambition. Yet there was a certain logic to its formal and enclosed style. The garden was laid out as a decorative backdrop to a new house in the Jacobean manner, built in 1884–91 by architects G. F. Bodley and Thomas Garner for Robert Windsor-Clive, a descendant of the Earls of Plymouth.

Lord Windsor had inherited an immense fortune on his coming of age, taking on the estates at St Fagan's, near Cardiff, and Oakley Park in Shropshire, as well as Hewell, set in a park with a 30-acre lake landscaped by Humphry Repton, near Redditch. With an income swelled by industrial development in South Wales as well as at Redditch, Lord Windsor was able to build and furnish his

Above: *A simple, four-square garden already existed on this site before the pink sandstone house was built in the 1880s.*

Left: *Seen from an upstairs window of the house, the elaborate floral beds and enclosures of the French garden, developed by the head gardener.*

houses lavishly, quite unlike many of his contemporaries, who were having to tighten their belts on their landed estates after the onset of agricultural depression.

So they abandoned the old Classical house by the lake, which was deemed too costly to repair, and up went magnificent Hewell Grange, of pink Cheshire sandstone from Runcorn, in another part of the grounds. It is an imposing, symmetrical composition with a decorative roof-line of Dutch-style gables, above which rise square turrets with pyramidal slate roofs. The site for the new house was chosen to align with an existing four-quartered garden of lawns and small flowerbeds which followed an attractive sweep downhill and up again. A central fountain enclosed by a circular water-lily pool was placed on the cross axis.

The head gardener, Andrew Pettigrew, was entrusted with developing the new gardens. This he did with great gusto, creating intricately patterned parterres, the beds edged with low box hedging in great swirls and arabesques. Flowerbeds were filled out with blocks of colour provided by summer bedding plants and herbaceous perennials in great variety, plus swathes of lilies and roses. Each of the four 'French' gardens was surrounded by a

serene frame of green turf; the screen enclosures and arches are recorded as being planted with trimmed limes. It was a confident scheme, skilfully executed, but perhaps we should not be surprised. Andrew Pettigrew was from a family of renowned gardeners: his father, Archibald Pettigrew, had charge of Cardiff Castle's grounds, and his brother was entrusted with the care of the ornamental parks of Cardiff and, later, Manchester.

No less impressive was Pettigrew's treatment of rising ground to the south-west of the house, carried out in 1900–03. Hewell Grange's great turf terraces were a magnificent feat of landscaping, crisp and enclosed by stepped yew hedging and with each level ascended to via a series of neat little turf steps, leading to a folly at the summit. Grander than the turf stairway at St Catherine's Court, and with a more leisurely progression than the steep stair of Milton Abbas in Dorset, their cool elegance is an inspired contrast to the ornate set-piece of the 'French' gardens. Around the same time, Pettigrew also added rose gardens and a maze.

Beyond the main set-piece, the grounds revealed a more Picturesque landscape, with little paths weaving through shrubberies and a dell devoted to ferns. There was, of course, a rock garden, complete with a centrepiece water-lily pool; also a clever 'swing stone' doorway, of crude stonework topped by a roughly executed Classical pediment, which, to modern eyes, conjures thoughts of Fred Flintstone rather than Salvator Rosa.

Mark Girouard has said of Hewell Grange that 'one can see the first freezing of the smile on the face of the country house, regarded as an independent architectural tradition. ... The great Victorian efflorescence of new and enlarged country houses had been a side-result of the growth of industry and the towns, and this same growth gradually toppled the country landowners from their position as leaders of the nation.' With its cavernous double-height hall, opulent and eclectic interiors, immense service wing and its use of the latest technological innovations (Hewell Grange was one of the first houses designed to be lit by electricity), it must have seemed that this was, to use a modern phrase, as good as it gets.

But it was not to last. The Countess of Plymouth wrote in 1932: 'Had we any idea how quickly the circumstances of life in the country ... would change, I do not think we should have dreamt of building a house of that size.'

The deprivations of the First World War dealt the first blow to Hewell Grange, and subsequently the house was too large and costly to run in the old style. After the Second World War the Plymouth family sold up, and for some years the house has been used as an open prison. Many garden features have disappeared and the French gardens have been turfed over, but castellated yew hedges mark their former position. Some restoration work to the lake and park is in progress, but the ornate grounds have had their day.

This turf stairway was perhaps the best example of its kind, creating a green but formal composition within the broader framework of Repton's park.

153

CLEEVE PRIOR MANOR, WORCESTERSHIRE

'The middle districts of England are rich in the natural graces of Nature, but they offer many examples also of the manner in which our ancestors fashioned their garden world,' advised *Country Life* in May 1900. 'In the villages some formal shape will start up from the hedge, confronting us with a strange presentation of bird or animal cut in box or yew. When we remember that the old English idea of a garden was an enclosed place, we begin to see how the hedge assumed its importance, what was the function of the terrace, and how necessary was the pleached alley.' Classic examples presented themselves in abundance, both in Cleeve Prior village and at its ancient manor house, close to the Warwickshire border. And it was indeed the extraordinary yew avenue that aroused *Country Life*'s enthusiasm for the gardens of Cleeve Prior Manor in 1900. Nobody knows precisely when the trees were planted, but their arrangement is unique, running in two evenly spaced rows

Above: *One side of the manor-house front. The sixteen great yews along the path were said to represent the twelve Apostles and four Evangelists.*

Left: *The entrance to Cleeve Prior. Lawrence Johnston admired the timber gates and had copies made for his garden at Hidcote Manor, not far away.*

from the front gate straight up to the Gothic-arched doorway of the stone house.

One prevailing story suggests that the yews – sixteen in all – had been planted to represent the twelve Apostles and four Evangelists, and there may be some truth in it, since, prior to the Dissolution, Cleeve Prior was attached to the powerful Abbey of Evesham; afterwards, it was handed to the dean and chapter of Worcester. Except during the years of Cromwell's Commonwealth, it remained in their ownership until 1859, when the manor passed to the Ecclesiastical Commission. When *Country Life* visited, the tenant was Mrs Holtum, a member of a local family, but ownership was still with the Church. The magazine devoted two features to the property, in May and June 1900, and Gertrude Jekyll wrote endearingly about it in *Some English Gardens* (1904), with George S. Elgood's evocative watercolours by way of illustration.

It is easy to see what so endeared Cleeve Prior to Miss Jekyll. The early seventeenth-century manor house at that time was a complete ensemble, surrounded by its farmyard and picturesque Cotswold-stone farm buildings. There were 'cart hovels' and stables across the yard in front of the prettily gated entrance; to one side lay the duckpond, haystacks and an ancient circular dovecote.

The little steps of a stone mounting block adjoined the low garden wall beside the gates. 'Those cart houses, with their lofty gables and external stairways leading to the lofts, have a singularly pictorial character, while the dove-cote is most interesting, and is probably not equalled in England.' All was set well back from the road and a little footpath ran from the manor to the church and up to the village green. Even in 1900 such timelessly bucolic scenes were becoming scarce and increasingly valued – by artists, at any rate – for their picturesqueness.

In front of the house, at either side of the yew alley there were simple lawns, one side with a border and old fruit trees, the other with small flowerbeds cut out of the turf. Elgood painted borders in the kitchen garden beside the manor, displaying a late-summer arrangement of sunflowers, marguerites, dahlias in scarlet and yellow, orange geums and lilac-coloured phlox in a cottagey, haphazard arrangement lining a grass path. Behind this was an

orchard and a small ornamental garden, but this is fertile, fruit-growing country on rising ground near the River Avon, and productivity appears always to have taken precedence over orna-ment. The survival of the simple old English garden down the centuries is no doubt due to the fact that this was a tenanted property; the expense of laying out fashionable new grounds was probably never considered.

Today, much has changed at Cleeve Prior, to the extent that it has recently been struck off English Heritage's list of important historic landscapes. Yet key elements have survived tenaciously and much can still be recognised beneath the veneer of modernity. Over the past twenty years the manor has been comprehensively split up. The house itself is now divided into three separate homes, each with its own garden; all of the remaining farm buildings have been converted into small houses. The old dovecote, now surrounded by a suburban-style private garden, has lost its sense of belonging to the larger landscape, but at least it is still intact, with a sound roof. The attractive timber gates dating from the eighteenth century (which were copied by Lawrence Johnston at Hidcote, not far away) are also still *in situ* above the original semicircular steps and well-worn flagstone path.

Left: *The great yews provided monumental garden architecture, framing a sequence of views including one of the adjacent dovecote.*

Below: *In 1900, Cleeve Prior Manor was still a working farm, a bucolic ensemble of circular dovecote, farmyard, hayricks, duckpond and cart hovels.*

HOAR CROSS, STAFFORDSHIRE

Occupying wooded and undulating countryside north of
Lichfield, the gardens of Hoar Cross were a gloriously elaborate
confection, tended by at least two dozen staff. Yet there appears an
almost unnatural stillness in *Country Life*'s photographs. There are
no gardeners trimming the hedges, no horses in harness, no ladies
with parasols taking a stroll through the grounds, and no boatmen
on the water. This lack of any sign of life appears at odds with the
brazen jollity of the bedded-out flowers and dancing fountains, but
there could be a reason for Hoar Cross's air of solitude. The
evidence suggests that, even if it was not the intention at the outset,
these formal and lavish grounds rapidly became a memorial garden.

The Hoar Cross estate had been bought in 1793 by Hugo
Meynell of Bradley (1759–1800), the eldest son of Hugo Meynell of
Quorndon (known as 'the father of foxhunting'). Young Hugo had
married an heiress in 1782, who brought with her several estates
including magnificent Temple Newsam, 'the Hampton Court of the
North', located near Leeds. With a handsome fortune at his
disposal, Hugo demolished the existing – though not very old –
house and built a new one (now known as the Old Hall), to serve
as an occasional hunting lodge. But he was not able to enjoy it for
long, as he died in 1800.

By the time it was the turn of his grandson, Hugo Francis
Meynell Ingram, to inherit the various properties in 1869, a new,
much smarter, seventy-roomed house by fashionable London
architect Henry Clutton was approaching completion within the
8,000-acre Hoar Cross estate. But following a serious hunting
injury, Hugo Francis died, preventing him from enjoying his
brand-new Jacobean-style mansion. In 1871, his childless thirty-
one-year-old widow, the Hon. Emily Charlotte, settled into the
house alone, having recently buried her fifty-year-old husband.
Emily, whose own family was wealthy (especially after the
discovery of the great Barnsley coalfield under their extensive
acres), inherited Temple Newsam and various other estates on her
husband's death, thus becoming one of the wealthiest independent
women in the country, though not without enduring the bitterness
of her husband's relatives.

Emily never remarried, and the gardens were laid out by her
head gardener, Mr Rowley, according to her instructions. The
photographs reveal a perfect Victorian interpretation of the pre-
Landscape-school pleasure gardens of the seventeenth century.
Indeed, her design is said to have been inspired by Francis Bacon's
1625 essay *Of Gardens*, with 'the main garden in the midst' and
'alleys on both sides'. Where the land gently falls away on the south
side of the house, a series of broad terraces spread outwards as far
as the ha-ha that separated the pleasure grounds from the park.

At Hoar Cross, hedges were cut with windows and swags, with
crenellated roofs here and ball finials there; two magnificent tunnels

*On the south side of the house, terraced formal gardens extended as far as the
ha-ha, which separated them from the park.*

were formed with pleached lime trees. By 1901, the tops of the level hedges were starting to reveal more elaborate topiary than Bacon would have countenanced, including mounted horses and an antlered stag, doubtless alluding to the Meynell family's connections with the hunt. The south gardens appear as a unified composition, but they were in the charge of rival senior gardeners. Mr Knight and Mr Dukes apparently did not get on, but perhaps it was the sheer competitiveness between these two that brought about the increasingly elaborate eruptions of topiary.

Emily Meynell Ingram was a pious woman. Upon her husband's death, she had commissioned the Gothic revivalist architect G. F. Bodley to build a church on high ground near the house. It was completed in 1876, at which time Hugo Francis's body was brought back to Hoar Cross from its place of rest at nearby Yoxall. (It was

Above: Within the formal enclosures, photographed in 1901. A topiary horse and rider is starting to take shape above the hedge in the distance.

Left: One of the pleached-lime walks, said to have been inspired by Francis Bacon's precept that a garden should have alleys on both sides.

observed that the prospects of potential staff at the house were considerably improved if they possessed a good singing voice to use in the church choir.)

The church's square, stone tower could be seen from almost anywhere in the gardens and its ubiquitous presence probably reinforced a sense that 'pagan' Classical garden sculpture would be inappropriate. Certainly, indoors, Emily's fine collection of seventeenth-century art was 'cleaned up' to avoid any suggestions of prurience; outdoors, even sheep could offend: ewes with suckling lambs had to be removed from the park beside the gardens so that Emily could stroll without embarrassment.

After Emily's death in 1904, Hoar Cross fared better than many estates, but it was not immune to the general shift in fortunes for landed families. By the Second World War, things had changed radically and much of the estate had been sold off. The house contents were sold in 1952, and in subsequent years the house changed hands several times, for a while housing a monastic community and later hosting 'medieval' banquets. Today, Hoar Cross has taken on a new life as a spa, amid simplified grounds.

STOKE EDITH, HEREFORDSHIRE

'Herrifordshire is like a fruitfull garden,' observed Celia Fiennes in her travel diary, published in 1698, during one of her many peripatetic tours of England in the late seventeenth and early eighteenth centuries. And Stoke Edith, between Ledbury and Hereford, was as scenic as any property in this fertile county.

The estate had been acquired of late by the Foley family, whose fortune was welded with iron, aided not least by the discovery of how to make nails with efficiency and economy. So an elegant new house was built at Stoke Edith in the late 1690s, replacing what Fiennes had a few years earlier described as 'a very good old house of Timber worke but old fashion'd and good roome for Gardens but all in an old form and mode ... Mr Folie intends to make both a new house and gardens; the latter I saw staked out.'

Exquisite needlework hangings for Stoke Edith (now in the Victoria and Albert Museum) show formal arrangements of topiary cones and grass plants, statues and fountains very much of the period. If that is how the gardens actually looked, then they must have been quite magnificent, but of course they did not survive through later fashions. For the Hon. Edward Foley, Humphry Repton produced a Red Book of recommended landscape improvements to the park in around 1792. Repton proposed earth movements to enhance the views of the deer park and the addition of copses and shrubberies. It seems that some, but not all, of his suggestions were carried out.

In 1903, *Country Life*'s photographs captured the surviving layout of a *parterre de broderie* and associated formal areas by the house, designed by W. A. Nesfield in 1854. The work had not been trouble-free: in 1857, Lady Emily Foley advised Nesfield that the blue gravel he had supplied as part of the pattern's infill had killed off her box hedging.

Lady Emily passed away, it is said, at the stroke of midnight, 31 December 1900 – the dawn of the new century. She could not have imagined that Stoke Edith itself would not last very much longer. The house caught fire in 1927 and later plans to rebuild were never fulfilled. A mere outline traces the original position of Nesfield's parterre and much of Repton's park has been ploughed up.

Above: *One of Nesfield's smaller parterres near the house, overshadowed by a magnificent cedar tree.*

Right: *The pattern of the parterre was marked out with dwarf box hedges and coloured gravels, with bedded-out flowers filling in the design.*

162

LILLESHALL, SHROPSHIRE

Wool, mining interests and a dash of Worcester sauce helped to create Lilleshall's gardens, on the fertile soils of the East Shropshire plain, near Telford.

In this historic landscape peppered with archaeological sites, the Roman military road of Watling Street carved its way westwards to the Welsh border, barely more than a mile south of Lilleshall Abbey. In medieval times, the abbey's estate covered some 30,000 acres and must have accumulated considerable wealth under the provisions of the Augustinian Order. But at least one abbot complained that the close proximity of the Roman road – a major highway in the Middle Ages – impoverished him by bringing too many hungry mouths to his door.

Henry VIII's Dissolution of the Monasteries put paid to any further calls on the abbey's charity, and subsequently the estate was reduced in size and the magnificent pink-stone church and its associated buildings at the water's edge began their descent into picturesque ruin. James Leveson Esq., whose family grew rich in the Wolverhampton wool trade, purchased Lilleshall in 1543. Through advantageous marriages and income from mining projects on the estate, the family's wealth and status rapidly advanced over the next few generations, with George Granville Leveson-Gower becoming the 1st Duke of Sutherland in 1833, the year of his death. His wife, already titled Countess Elizabeth of Sutherland in her own right, thus became widely known as 'the Duchess-Countess'. It was this generation who commissioned Wyattville to build a new, more fashionable home, replacing a mid-eighteenth-century hall in the village; it was completed in 1829.

Fine Italianate gardens followed, with broad walks and balustrades, much of the work having been directed by Duchess Harriet, wife of the 2nd Duke. Interested in both the house and its gardens, she took copious notes when visiting other properties and incorporated the bits that she approved of into the grounds of Lilleshall, with some success.

A promenade terrace was wrapped around the hall, with stone stairways leading to 28 acres of spacious pleasure grounds, within a

Above: *One of Lilleshall's most celebrated features: the 200-yard Apple Walk of espaliered trees on an iron framework.*

Left: *The promenade terrace with stone stairways leading down to the flower gardens. Labour-intensive strips of turf lined the paths.*

scenic estate covering about 600 acres. The main view looked on to concentric circular beds erupting in blazes of summer colour. In 1898, it was noted that the bedded-out calceolarias were thriving – 'the more noteworthy because disease has attacked this once favourite flower within recent years, throwing it partly out of cultivation in many places'.

There were also zonal pelargoniums, nurtured in the glasshouses in great quantity, and the latest hybrid strains of compact tuberous begonias, bred to deliver flowers borne well above the leaves in brilliant shades of orange, scarlet, crimson, buff and white. Standard roses were arranged like lollipops, at regular intervals around the beds of a terrace on the next level down. The landscape beyond was well wooded with magnificent trees, but a view was cut through them so that the romantic spectacle of the abbey ruins could be seen from the house. From the windows of the library a vista focused on a 70-foot obelisk, erected on the summit of Lilleshall Hill in 1833 in memory of the 1st Duke.

Country Life's interest in the gardens of Lilleshall coincided with the tenure of the 4th Duke of Sutherland, who used the house only as a shooting lodge since he had, among his several properties, the grander Trentham nearby. Even so, it was observed in 1897 that the Duke had only recently, at great cost, constructed a magnificent drive 2 miles long, so that the house could be reached from the main turnpike road. It was used for the first time when the Prince of Wales paid a visit to the abbey woods and 'had a big day's shooting, considerably over 1,000 head of game being bagged'.

One of the most celebrated features of Lilleshall's gardens was the Apple Walk, stretching for nearly 200 yards in a brilliantly executed tunnel, believed to have been the longest of its kind in the country. Its many scores of espaliered trees were pretty with blossoms in spring, provided a shady walk through the summer, and climaxed in a brilliant finale of abundant well-flavoured fruits from late summer until the onset of winter.

Beyond the Apple Walk lay the rose garden, where nineteen or more beds were filled with the fashionable bush roses of the day, including 'Alfred Colomb', 'Baroness Rothschild', 'Beauty of Waltham', 'Captain Christy', 'Margaret Dickson', 'Mrs John Laing', 'Merveille de Lyon', 'La France', 'Lady Helen Stewart', 'Rêve d'Or' and 'Lord Macaulay'. Over the walls romped 'Garland', 'Felicité Perpetuée', the 'Dundee' rambler and 'garish'

'Crimson' rambler – 'than which few roses are more brilliant'. Another feature of the gardens was its collection of sweet violets, nurtured in cold frames for gathering into posies, and bearing names that conjure up a forgotten age: 'Victoria Regina', 'Princess Beatrice'; fashionable American cultivars such as 'New York' and 'California'; also the deeply fragrant, coveted Parma violets of the Levant, including double-flowered 'Marie Louise', which was probably named for the wife of Napoleon Bonaparte.

The 4th Duke died in 1913, and following the outbreak of the First World War, his son and heir decided to retrench at home, selling off the Trentham Estate, plus some 250 acres of Lilleshall, though in the short term he retained the hall itself and 50 acres of gardens. These, too, he sold in 1917, and in 1927 Lilleshall was bought by Herbert Ford, a local businessman whose wealth had come from the Ironbridge gorge and his wife's inheritance, she being a Perrin, of Lea and Perrin's Worcester sauce.

Ford tapped early into the heritage industry, opening the hall at Lilleshall and its grounds to paying visitors who flocked there to wander through the lavish gardens, take rides on a narrow-gauge railway down to the abbey ruins, and join tea dances in Ford Hall, the converted stable block that the proprietor had made into a ballroom. And he stopped at nothing to get the crowds in; a few judiciously placed advertisements announcing that the *Hindenberg* airship would be flying over the estate satisfactorily boosted the numbers one summer. Once the crowds were assembled, Ford read out a telegram he had sent to himself declaring that, due to bad weather, the flight of the *Hindenberg* had had to be rerouted and would not be taking place after all.

During the Second World War, the pleasure gardens were closed and Cheltenham Ladies College was moved to Lilleshall; afterwards the house was briefly used as an orphanage for Barnardo's. The next big step for Lilleshall came in 1949, when it was selected as a National Recreation Centre to serve the north of England. Ford sold the hall along with 10 acres for £33,000 and made further gifts of land and money to the sporting organisation in exchange for continuing to live in the house. The centre's moment of fame came in 1966 when the England football team trained there for two weeks prior to their World Cup victory.

Over recent decades, since Lilleshall became the National Sports Centre, residential blocks and sports training halls have smothered part of the grounds. Some remnants of the gardens have clung on tenaciously. There are still circular beds on the lawn, though they are not the labour-intensive creations of Lilleshall's heyday. A path survives where the Apple Walk once was, taking in part of its route. A substantial chunk of the park is now a golf course, and Telford town is knocking at the gates, having crept outwards along the Newport road. The abbey ruins, a little way off, are cared for by English Heritage in a setting of peaceful lawns and great yew trees.

The flower gardens. The Apple Walk can be seen on the far right; on the left, a view cut through the trees displays the Lilleshall Abbey ruins.

SEVEN

THE NORTH

Stuck in the past and slow to catch up with the freer styles arriving with the twentieth century, the great northern gardens were made to last – at least for a few more decades, until the First World War finally made them untenable. The lake at Heslington Hall (*left*) was an enlargement of an ancient canal beside topiaries planted in around 1710. At Crewe Hall in Cheshire (*below*), Nesfield had created, in the mid-nineteenth century, a terraced walk between little parterres, plus another, much larger parterre stretching up to a lake on the north side. Nesfield's work also continued to thrive at Stanwick, Yorkshire, and in the walled gardens of Alnwick, Northumberland – both projects having been created half a century earlier, for the 4th Duke of Northumberland.

A voracious demand for new plants was met by Backhouse Nurseries of York, a business founded in 1815 whose own demise was hastened by the Great War and its effect on gardens nationwide.

ALNWICK CASTLE, NORTHUMBERLAND

Medieval Alnwick Castle, amid the gently rolling hills of Northumberland close to the Scottish border, sits within an idyllic park laid out by Capability Brown. Its 12-acre eighteenth-century walled garden occupies a sloping site 300 yards from the frowning stone castle, and for many years it lay forlorn and forgotten until a remarkable renaissance began in 1996. It is now becoming one of the most famous and glamorous gardens in the country, after decades of neglect; in an age when exotic fruits are flown in from around the world and armies of garden staff are no longer needed to provide a huge range of crops for several large households, these old walled grounds need to find new uses, though no other has been as lavishly laid out as the current project to revive Alnwick.

The 'lost' walled garden reached its zenith in the nineteenth century, during the time of Algernon, the 4th Duke of Northumberland. A Royal Navy veteran who had served in the French wars from 1804 to 1815, he had been elevated to the peerage in 1816, becoming Baron Prudhoe. Prior to his years at Alnwick, Algernon had spent a good deal of time at Stanwick Park in Yorkshire (pages 176–9), and he always invested in both of these properties, making substantial house improvements, rebuilding the farmhouses and estate cottages and enhancing the gardens. No doubt there was plenty of exchange of plants between Alnwick and Stanwick during the time of the 4th Duke, who employed Nesfield to lay out the formal gardens at both properties. The Nesfield parterres at Alnwick were on a colossal scale, with dwarf box hedges enclosing raised flowerbeds and gravelled areas, while slender stone edgings separated paths from marginal strips of turf.

When *Country Life* photographed Alnwick's walled garden in the late 1890s, it still had the mid-Victorian layout implemented during the 4th Duke's lifetime. Rows of glasshouses were leaned against south-facing walls in the lower end, and the vista focused on an elegant conservatory erected in 1862. A series of patterned flowerbeds, decorated with seasonal bedding plants brought on in the hothouses, provided an element of high ornament in the centre of an area that was also intensively productive.

Nemesis for Alnwick's old walled garden came in the shape of two World Wars – particularly the Second, when the garden was ploughed up for the Dig For Victory campaign, assisted by local volunteers and Land Army recruits. Afterwards, part of it was used as a tree nursery, while the elegant infrastructure of glasshouses, stone-edged walks and a water basin went into steep decline.

This is one lost garden that appears to have a great future, for the present Duchess of Northumberland has invested in lavish water gardens by the Belgian designers Jacques and Peter Wirtz and further ornamental grounds are currently under construction. Overall, the Alnwick project, dubbed 'the Versailles of the North', is expected to cost around £42 million.

The mid-nineteenth-century formal flowerbeds within the 12-acre walled garden, with extensive glasshouses and a fine central conservatory.

CREWE HALL, CHESHIRE

The name of Crewe these days is inextricably linked with a large railway station in the south Cheshire plain, but that famously busy junction (and the industrial town which grew around it) was named after the Crewe family, which traced its roots back to Anglo-Saxon times. Construction of the present mansion of Crewe Hall was begun in 1615 for Sir Randolph Crewe; it was a substantial and elaborate project that was to last for twenty-one years.

No doubt a suitably formal garden was concurrently laid out beside the magnificent Jacobean house, though it would have been swept away by a later generation; certainly for some while there was no shortage of attention paid to beautifying the park. Capability Brown installed a magnificent lake, which at one time extended for over 50 acres. In his *Tour* of 1768 Lord Verulam noted that 'the three fronts [of the house] look into a park which has been admirably laid out by Mr. Brown'. William Emes is recorded as making further alterations to the park in 1769 and both John Webb and Humphry Repton are credited with working at Crewe, probably in the 1790s, though Repton's Red Book has not been found. Repton had been staying with John Crewe MP and his wife in May 1791 when he wrote a few lines in their album, beginning: 'Thus it happens at Crewe, where, tho' Taste overflows, One Repton's called in to display what he knows.'

Above: *Urns, pinnacles and assorted stone animals enlivened the garden stairways beside the seventeenth-century mansion.*

Right: *The north view towards Capability Brown's great lake, which was drained during the Second World War.*

Following pages: *Nesfield's parterre of the 1850s, leading to a statue of Neptune at the water's edge. By 1901, the box hedges looked threadbare in places and the style had passed out of fashion.*

But the climactic moment for Crewe's formal gardens came when Nesfield entered the scene a couple of generations later, just prior to Charles Barry's extensive renovations to the house, which caught fire in 1866. William Andrews Nesfield (1793–1881) had had an army career – he served in the Peninsular War under Wellington – and subsequently became a painter of some note before turning his artistic skills to designing gardens from the 1840s onwards. Whereas his paintings demonstrate a freely romantic and Picturesque quality in the spirit of J. M. W. Turner and G. F. Robson (he was a member of the Old Watercolour Society for nearly thirty years), the parterre designs of his later career demonstrate an oddly contrasting devotion to precise symmetry. Perhaps he was merely reinterpreting the rigorous sense of discipline that must have made him an able soldier. At any rate, Nesfield's 'gardens of embroidery' were in great demand through the 1850s and 1860s, following the successful creation of formal gardens at Kew, Holkham, Balcarres and Castle Howard among others; in Cheshire alone he carried out substantial commissions at Dorfold Hall, Arley Hall and Eaton Hall, as well as at Crewe (though none of them survive).

Nesfield's design for Crewe Hall's North Parterre, published in colour in a supplement to the *Gardeners' Chronicle* in February 1863, demonstrates his mastery of balanced scrolls and curlicues to be traced out in little box hedges, and also his devotion to coloured gravels. Clearly, this (and a smaller parterre laid out on a flat lawned terrace on the east side) comes from the same stable as the parterre at Stoke Edith (page 163). It makes one wonder whether the Crewe family experienced similar difficulties with the gravels that had troubled Lady Emily Foley's garden: the accidental demise of the Stoke Edith box hedges due to artificially coloured stones leaching lead or other poisons into the earth must have been repeated at more than one of his great parterres of the period.

Notwithstanding the high esteem in which Nesfield was held in the 1850s and 1860s, his reputation was not to last beyond his lifetime. By the 1880s, a critic had noted that Crewe Hall's parterre 'hardly strikes one as a garden; it is rather an appendage to the house itself, adding to its stateliness, and recalling, by its prevailing colours of buff and blue, the old traditions of the family'. And in the 1901 *Country Life* article, Charles Latham defensively advised, 'There is formality in the regular shapes of the bedding, and some may quarrel with the character; but let us recognise that there is merit in this style as in any other.'

The Crewe parterres survived, after a fashion, until the Second World War, when the estate was occupied by the War Office. The parterres were grassed over and the lake was drained and turned into meadow. The Crewe family had moved out in 1922, and, with no heir to the title, Lord Crewe had offered the Hall and adjacent estates to Cheshire County Council, which declined them. In 1936, the house and most of its land were bought by the Duchy of Lancaster, and in 1998 it was sold again. Crewe Hall now thrives once more, but this time as a country-house hotel, in modestly lawned grounds with beautiful trees.

STANWICK PARK, YORKSHIRE

Stanwick Park was situated in the northern Yorkshire Dales between the Rivers Swale and Tees, an area that was (and arguably still is) the most captivating landscape in the county, traced with its dry-stone-walled fields and little stone barns. Stanwick itself was so deeply loved by its owner throughout the second half of the nineteenth century that its rapid demise seems all the more tragic.

From 1865, it was the permanent home of Eleanor, the dowager Duchess of Northumberland, until her death forty-six years later. In that time, she made significant improvements to the estate and its gardens, about which she was very knowledgeable. *Country Life*'s photographs were taken in the high summer of 1899 and show immaculately cared-for pleasure grounds within a scenic deer park studded with magnificent trees of oak, ash, elm, beech, sweet chestnut and even walnut.

The main entrance to the park was way off to the east, close to the pretty village of Aldbrough. A long carriage drive swept westwards to the house, and on entering the park, the northerly view to the right, framed by enormous trees, took in the mound of Henall Hill with its ancient earthworks at the summit. A little farther on, views opened out on to the attractive manor house of Kirkbridge and the restored ancient church of St John. The southerly prospect took in more parkland views, including finely disported copses, said to be the work of William Gilpin some time in the last quarter of the eighteenth century.

So, up you would sweep in your carriage to the house – and it would only be the horse-drawn kind, for Duchess Eleanor loathed the invention of motorcars and forbade their presence in her park. From an inner lodge, wrought-iron gates led into the pleasure gardens. The straight drive continued through fine lawns, on the north side bordered by rhododendrons and other shrubs, behind which lay the walled gardens.

The house was more or less square in plan, with an open court at its heart – not unlike the arrangement at Syon House, the Northumberlands' home near London. Classically austere Stanwick Hall had been built in various stages, the south side bearing the date 1662 and the west 1740. The north and east blocks of 1842 were the work of Decimus Burton, the architect of the palm house at Kew Gardens. An 'Italian' garden had been created beside the main entrance to the south, entered via exquisite wrought-iron gates designed by the architect Anthony Salvin. This garden was the creation of W. A. Nesfield, who, from 1843, had worked closely with Burton at Kew. He provided a formal and uncluttered setting from which the beauty of Stanwick's grounds could be viewed beyond a stonework balustrade. Its main focus was a fine fountain of Aberdeen granite, either side of which stood tall reproductions of the Borghese and Medici vases planted with the large, spiny succulent *Agave americana* Variegata.

The fishpond north-west of Stanwick Hall. The house became a convalescent home in 1914, following the Duchess of Northumberland's death in 1911.

East of the house lay the rigorously managed walled gardens. Nearest was the square French garden, an embroidery pattern of beds interwoven with crunchy gravel paths. This interesting area was devised by a French *abbé*, an *émigré* during the French Revolution who was domiciled for a while at Stanwick. Hedges of dwarf box lined beds that had been packed, by the late nineteenth century, with herbaceous plants in great variety, including phlox, dahlias, Japanese anemones and helianthus; other small beds were entirely devoted to fragrant heliotrope. And here were the Stanwick carnations: 'the famous misnamed Raby Castle', actually brought to Stanwick many years earlier by the Duchess from her sister-in-law's home, Lebanon House, at Twickenham.

The garden's southern wall was arcaded in order to exchange views with the park, but in the middle of that wall was a delightful conceit: an ornamental dairy, octagonal in shape and with a finely decorated interior; its floor was inlaid with Indian marble, soap-stone, agate and cornelian from Agra. At the opposite end was a magnificent conservatory nurturing exotics.

Adjoining the *abbé*'s creation was the larger walled kitchen garden. It was a traditionally four-quartered arrangement, which had a long range of glasshouses along the south-facing wall.

Cosseted in their warmth were peaches, grapes, figs and nectarines, including the Stanwick nectarine, raised from stones brought back from Aleppo, Syria, and said to yield the largest and finest-flavoured fruits then known. All of this, plus further kitchen gardens at the Duchess's adjoining estate of Carlton Hall (which had an ice house), was managed by her dedicated head gardener, William Higgie, who had been in charge since 1866.

The Duchess, an active and benevolent landlord, died in 1911, aged ninety-one, and was mourned by all her tenants. During the First World War, Stanwick Hall became a convalescent home for the wounded. Carlton Hall housed German prisoners of war and was subsequently demolished in 1919. Stanwick was sold to speculators in 1921 to finance death duties following the demise of the 7th Duke. The estates were promptly divided and sold off; Gilpin's magnificent trees and other woodlands were ruthlessly felled. Elegant Stanwick Hall itself was demolished in 1923, and everything that could be sold was.

Above: *William Higgie, head gardener, in the garden designed by a French* abbé*, with the conservatory and adjacent orchid house at the back.*

Right: *Nesfield's formal Italian garden beside the main entrance. The carriage drive and avenue are visible beyond the balustrade.*

BACKHOUSE NURSERIES, YORKSHIRE

'Whatever the size or situation of your garden, if arranged on the Backhouse design, it will be a perennial dream of beauty for years to come,' claimed a 1909 advertisement in *Country Life* for the nursery James Backhouse & Son. This was one of the most famous of nineteenth-century nurseries, though today its legacy is obscure.

James Backhouse (1794–1869) was a Quaker missionary and gardener whose career among the plants began at Wagstaffe's Nursery in Norwich. In 1815, he and his brother, Thomas, bought the long-established nursery of George Telford in York, and a horticultural dynasty was born. By 1821, their catalogue listed huge quantities of ornamental plants, trees and fruits, including 163 varieties of gooseberry and 126 different apples.

On 3 September 1831, James Backhouse, aged thirty-seven and a widower, embarked on a mission to Australia. He was away for a

Above: *A century ago, more than 100 acres were cultivated for nursery stock.*

Left: *The handsome entrance to the Holgate nursery near the city of York.*

Following pages (left): *A display of lilies and juvenile Norfolk Island pine trees in one of the nursery's many glasshouses;* (right): *The underground fernery, whose collections inspired E. J. Lowe to publish the two-volume study* Our Native Ferns *in 1865–67.*

few months short of ten years, but during that time he collected and sent back to England the seeds of many Australasian plants, which were propagated at the nursery and also at Kew.

Two more generations of Backhouses (both called James) ran the nursery through the nineteenth and early twentieth centuries, during which time they further increased its huge range of plants and moved premises a couple of times. The photographs reproduced here were taken during the great years of the Holgate nursery at York, where over 100 acres were cultivated, including forty glasshouses. Alpines and ferns were specialities; a 'miniature Switzerland' rock garden was built using 1,500 tons of stone.

Large nurseries were badly affected by the First World War. Gardens had been changed forever, as great houses lacked the staff or funds to maintain them. The third-generation James Backhouse reluctantly sold off much of the land, and in 1921 the remaining business was bought by the Hamilton family, which ran it until 1945. The rock garden declined and was demolished by York Corporation, and in 1955 the plant collections were sold off in a two-day auction. Eponymous plants include *Erica carnea* James Backhouse, the dainty, bell-flowered *Correa backhouseana* (collected at Cape Grim, on the coast of Tasmania), and several rare orchids.

HESLINGTON HALL, YORKSHIRE

At Heslington, on the south-eastern edge of the city of York, a prim topiary garden of the early 1700s was refashioned over a period of two hundred years into something much more imposing, in grounds that survived against the odds until the 1960s.

But the story starts much earlier, for Heslington Hall was built in 1568 as a country house for Thomas Eymes Esq., a member of Queen Elizabeth's council for the northern part of England – an administration formed by Henry VIII. Eymes had a role in redistributing the ecclesiastical properties and estates that had been seized in the Reformation. Along the way, he acquired several estates and considerable wealth for himself, and proceeded to build himself a great house at Heslington.

Eymes died in 1578, and in 1601 the property was sold to Sir Thomas Hesketh, who built a hospital nearby for 'eight poor men and one poor woman over 50 years old and of good name'. But neither was Hesketh able to enjoy the elegant mansion for long, for he died in 1605, whereupon the estate stayed with a succession of Hesketh descendants over another hundred years until it passed, by marriage, to James Yarburgh in 1708, and the creation of the gardens began.

James Yarburgh (1644–1730) was a man of means and social stature: he had been a godson and page of honour to James II, a lieutenant-colonel in the Foot Guards, and aide-de-camp to the Duke of Marlborough. He therefore required an appropriately important garden and, though he was already sixty-four years old when he came to Heslington, he lived into extreme old age (for the time) and had more than two decades ahead of him to oversee development of the grounds.

Three walled gardens were laid out beside the Elizabethan house. The two closest to the house were planted with yew obelisks in around 1710, in a formal manner that had prevailed during Yarburgh's lifetime but was rapidly heading out of fashion. But Yarburgh was of an older generation and not under pressure to follow at Heslington the new 'natural' style already being advocated by Ashley Cooper and Joseph Addison, which would sweep away the majority of formal gardens as the century progressed.

The third walled area is believed to have been a kitchen garden. Yarburgh is also credited with building a double-storey gazebo, whose first-floor viewing room overlooked a T-shaped canal stretching out into the park. (The ensemble bears comparison with the contemporary 'Dutch' garden of Westbury Court, Gloucestershire, which has been restored by the National Trust.)

It was fortunate that Yarburgh's gardens survived for a century following his death, for by the time it was the turn of the sixty-six-year-old bachelor Yarburgh Graeme to inherit the estate in 1852, formal gardens were back in vogue and Heslington's was already mature, dressed in compelling yew topiary. Those yews were not,

In the late nineteenth century, cones of variegated holly were added to the ancient yews. The tower pinnacles on the house were removed in 1903.

of course, the simple obelisks of James Yarburgh's day. As the belt of a portly gentleman needs to be loosened a notch with every passing year, topiary gradually fattens out with the passing of time and new shapes present themselves to the artistic gardener. In the nineteenth century, the topiary was variously said to represent a chess set and even the Twelve Apostles – an interpretation that has also been (more reasonably) applied to the ancient topiaries of Packwood House, Warwickshire, and Cleeve Prior, Worcestershire.

Yarburgh Graeme (who took on the surname Yarburgh, thus becoming known as Yarburgh Yarburgh) commissioned P. C. Hardwicke, architect of the Great Hall at Euston Station, to alter the house, relandscape the front entrance and add slate-tiled spires to the staircase towers overlooking the gardens. A new stable block was created and the mansion was enlarged to 109 rooms. In reworking the grounds to Victorian tastes, a rectangular fishpond was filled in and a new terrace created, while the formal canal of the

park was refashioned into a scenic boating lake of irregular shape. A boathouse and dovecote were also added, but Yarburgh, like some of his predecessors at Heslington, was unable to enjoy the new developments, dying in 1856 after a prolonged illness.

When *Country Life* featured Heslington Hall in 1900, two centuries of care had produced remarkable topiary gardens surrounded by neat gravel paths and groups of bedded-out variegated pelargoniums. Carefully trimmed ivy clothed the two-storey eighteenth-century gazebo, the house and many of the estate cottages. Pathside pots were filled with striped agaves – admired for their sculptural foliage, but bearing vicious spines primed to gash any unwary passers-by.

By 1903, fashions had altered again and the tower pinnacles were removed. Staffing was affected by the First World War, and during the Second World War the Hall was occupied by RAF Bomber Command, with the regiment staying on until 1952 when the property was sold. Heslington Hall and a large slice of the grounds became the University of York in 1962. Since then, large areas of the park have been covered by campus buildings, though the lake has been retained, as well as the – now gigantic – topiaries which are approaching three hundred years in age.

Above: *By 1900, the topiaries were nearly two hundred years old. Iron-railed steps led to the upper storey of the gazebo, seen at the end of this vista.*

Left: *Trimming the great yews. In the foreground, ivy smothers the two-storey gazebo, believed to date from c.1710, which overlooked a canal.*

HIGHHEAD CASTLE, CUMBERLAND

Highhead Castle was defined by its setting, still widely regarded as one of the most romantic and dramatic locations in England, at the eastern extremities of the Lake District. It was built towering over a cliff, 100 feet above the noisily busy waters of the River Ive, which carves its way through a leafy gorge.

A century ago, 24 acres of pleasure grounds surrounded the house. Built of local red sandstone in 1744–48, its isolated and thrilling location appealed to the Picturesque sensibilities of the eighteenth century, though earlier buildings on the site had been erected for strategic purposes.

The eighteenth-century house, built for Henry Richmond Brougham, Sheriff of Cumberland, was revered for the high quality of the stone carvings decorating its exterior, for which skilled craftsmen were imported from Italy; construction costs were said to have amounted to 10,000 Hanoverian sovereigns – more than £50 million in today's terms. It was regarded as the finest house of its period in Cumberland, with magnificent plasterwork and woodcarvings in the interior and elegant Venetian windows that took in splendid views, especially to the south.

The approach was via a long, straight lane on the north side, with the gravelled carriage drive encircling a serene stretch of lawn. West of the lawn, an avenue of pleached limes acted as a screen in front of the handsome stable block. On the east side, fastigiate yews stood sentinel at the top of a stone stairway descending into the gardens. Here, the hill dropping away to the south was carved into a series of three turf terraces, bringing a little order into the landscape above the beech woods and the beck. The rectangular rose beds and simple topiaries were not sophisticated, but had a rustic simplicity that suited the natural beauty of the place.

'The garden and the romantic surroundings ... lend a grandeur and charm hardly surpassed by Houghton or, we may conjecture, by Strawberry Hill,' wrote Christopher Hussey in 1921. A token of formality amid the Picturesque grandeur could be seen in the entrance court to the north, with its imposing gates copied from a pair at Canons Ashby in Northamptonshire. Guarded by a pair of dragon-winged sphinxes atop impressive stone piers, the double-stairway grand entrance was reached by a flagstone path leading through a neat little parterre garden, edged with dwarf box and infilled with roses.

Highhead went through several changes of ownership and fortune in the twentieth century, but in December 1956 a fire broke out in one of the bedrooms in the afternoon, and by the next day the house was a sooty black skeleton. Various plans have surfaced over the years to demolish or restore the building, but so far none has been taken up, and the house remains a tragic shell among wild, overgrown grounds, but still in a majestic setting.

Lawned terraces led steeply down to the beck. The north entrance front of the castle can be seen beyond the garden wall, as can the sphinx-topped gate piers.

The *Country Life* archive, begun in 1897, has been a key source of reference and has provided all the photographs. Other helpful sources include: the Royal Horticultural Society's journal, 1866 onwards; the *Gardeners' Chronicle*, 1841 onwards; *Garden History*, the Garden History Society's journal, newsletters and papers; and relevant files held by England's County Records Offices. Another, more unusual source has been Valerie Martin's historical record of life in Findon village at her website: www.findonvillage.com.

Aslet, Clive, *The Last Country Houses*, Yale University Press, New Haven and London, 1982.

Blomfield, Reginald and Thomas, F. Inigo, *The Formal Garden in England*, Macmillan, London, 1892.

Brown, Jane, *The Art and Architecture of English Gardens*, Weidenfeld & Nicolson, London, 1989.

—, *Eminent Gardeners*, Viking, London, 1990.

Collett-White, A. and J., *Gunnersbury Park and the Rothschilds*, Heritage Publications, Hounslow, Middlesex, 1993.

Colley, Alfred, *Heslington: A Portrait of the Village*, Neville Publishing, Heslington, Yorkshire, 1992.

Du Cane, Ella and Florence, *The Flowers and Gardens of Japan*, A. & C. Black, London, 1908.

Elgood, G. S. and Jekyll, G., *Some English Gardens*, Longmans, London, 1904.

Elias, Gillian, *The Rose King*, Nottinghamshire County Council, Nottingham, 1994.

Elliott, Brent, *The Country House Garden: From the Archives of Country Life*, Mitchell Beazley, London, 1995.

—, *Victorian Gardens*, B. T. Batsford, London, 1986.

Evans, Gareth, *Hoar Cross Hall, Staffordshire: Portrait of a Victorian Country House*, Stowefields Publications, Stafford, 1994.

Festing, Sally, *Gertrude Jekyll*, Viking, London, 1991.

Fleming, Laurence and Gore, Alan, *The English Garden*, Michael Joseph, London, 1979.

Girouard, Mark, *The Victorian Country House*, rev. edn, Yale University Press, New Haven and London, 1979.

Hadfield, Miles, *Topiary and Ornamental Hedges*, A. & C. Black, London, 1971.

Hall, Michael, *The English Country House 1897–1939: From The Archives of Country Life*, Mitchell Beazley, London, 1994; reprinted 2001 by Aurum Press.

Hole, Samuel Reynolds, *The Memories of Dean Hole*, E. Arnold, London, 1892.

Holme, Charles (editor), *The Gardens of England in the Midland and Eastern Counties*, The Studio, London, 1908.

Huxley, Anthony, *An Illustrated History of Gardening*, Paddington Press (for the Royal Horticultural Society), New York and London, 1978.

— and Griffiths, Mark (editors), *The New Royal Horticultural Society Dictionary of Gardening*, Macmillan, London, 1992.

Jacques, David, *Georgian Gardens*, B. T. Batsford, London, 1983.

Jekyll, Gertrude, *Garden Ornament*, George Newnes (for *Country Life*), London, 1918.

— and Weaver, Lawrence, *Gardens for Small Country Houses*, George Newnes (for *Country Life*), London, 1912.

Jellicoe, Sir Geoffrey, Jellicoe, Susan, Goode, Patrick and Lancaster, Michael, *The Oxford Companion to Gardens*, Oxford University Press, Oxford, 1986.

Lacey, Stephen, *Gardens of the National Trust*, The National Trust, London, 1996.

Lord, Tony (editor), *The RHS Plant Finder*, Dorling Kindersley, London, 1993.

Lutyens (Hayward Gallery exhibition catalogue), Arts Council of Great Britain, London, 1981.

Musgrave, Toby, Gardner, Chris and Musgrave, Will, *The Plant Hunters*, Ward Lock, London, 1998.

Ottewill, David, *The Edwardian Garden*, Yale University Press, New Haven and London, 1989.

Pankhurst, Alex, *Who Does Your Garden Grow?*, Earl's Eye Publishing, Colchester, Essex, 1992.

Pugsley, Steven, *Devon Gardens: An Historical Survey*, Sutton, Stroud, 1994.

Pulham, James, *Picturesque Ferneries and Rock Garden Scenery*, 1877.

Quest-Ritson, Charles, *The English Garden: A Social History*, Viking, London, 2001.

Rackham, Oliver, *Trees and Woodland in the British Landscape*, rev. edn, Dent, London, 1990.

Robinson, John Martin, *A Guide to the Country Houses of the North West*, Constable, London, 1991.

Robinson, William, *The English Flower Garden*, 9th edn, John Murray, London, 1905.

Rothschild, Miriam, Garton, Kate and de Rothschild, Lionel, *The Rothschild Gardens*, Gaia Books, London, 1996.

Sandon, Eric, *Suffolk Houses*, Baron Publishing, Woodbridge, Suffolk, 1977.

Strong, Roy, *Country Life 1897–1997: The English Arcadia*, Country Life Books, London, 1996.

—, *The Renaissance Garden in England*, Thames & Hudson, London, 1979.

Stroud, Dorothy, *Capability Brown*, Faber & Faber, London, 1975.

Symes, Michael, *Fairest Scenes: Five Great Surrey Gardens*, Elmbridge Museum Service, Elmbridge, Surrey, 1988.

Thacker, Christopher, *The Genius of Gardening*, Weidenfeld & Nicolson, London, 1994.

Thomas, Graham Stuart, *The Rock Garden and its Plants*, Dent, London, 1989.

Triggs, F. Inigo, *Formal Gardens of England and Scotland*, B. T. Batsford, London, 1902

Weaver, Lawrence, *Houses and Gardens by E. L. Lutyens*, George Newnes (for *Country Life*), London, 1913.

Wheater, W., *Some Historic Mansions of Yorkshire*, Richard Jackson, Leeds, 1888.

Worsley, Giles, *England's Lost Houses: From The Archives of Country Life*, Aurum Press, 2002.